SOME STUFF

I WISH MY DAD HAD TOLD ME

LIFE, LOVE & MONEY ... THE A~~WF~~UL TRUTH AWESOME

ERROL BRAITHWAITE

ISBN 978-0-6397-9122-7 (print)
ISBN 978-0-6397-9123-4 (e-book)

Cover photo by Oliver Sjöström
www.pexels.com

Stock images from stock.adobe.com

Book Design by Liza Mijburgh
www.pixelpingdesign.co.za

Disclaimer: The contents of this book are provided for informational purposes only. The author, publisher, and sellers have made reasonable efforts to ensure the accuracy and completeness of the information presented in this book. However, they make no representations or warranties of any kind, express or implied, regarding the completeness, accuracy, reliability, or suitability of the information contained herein.

The reader acknowledges that the information provided in this book is based on the author's personal experiences, research, and understanding, and that individual results and outcomes may vary. The author, publisher, and sellers shall not be held liable for any damages howsoever arising out of the reader's reliance on the information provided in this book.

The author, publisher, and sellers shall not be responsible in any way for the outcomes of any actions taken by the reader based on the contents of this book. The reader assumes full responsibility for the use of the information contained herein.

For my dear children, Thomas, Duncan and Hannah and their wonderful partners. May this collection of signposts be of some use to you as you navigate the awesome world of adulthood.

To my dearest wife, Megan, thank you for noticing me in high school and for sticking with me all these years. What a privilege to be married to such a wise, loving, fun soulmate for so many years.

And thank you to my parents, Gill and Doug and my sister Jocelyn, who set an example of love and kindness and integrity that I deeply admire and cherish.

To those many friends who gave so much inspiration and encouragement in the writing of this book, and who even proofread some of the drafts. Megan McMurray, Dr Martin Pohlmann, Angela de Longchamps, Trevor Johnston, Stephen Pohlmann, and my wife and children—thank you.

BUY THIS BOOK

To buy this book and all the others referenced in it, visit **www.some-stuff.co**

SOME STUFF
I WISH MY DAD HAD TOLD ME

(Well okay, maybe he did)

Two old Irishmen are sitting in a bar:
Paddy says "I wish I had listened to me
Dad when I was a teenager."
Patrick says, "Why? What did he say?"
Paddy replies, "I don't know. I wasn't listening."

ROUTE MAP

RED PILL OR BLUE PILL?

If you saw the classic movie The Matrix starring Keanu Reeves (1999), you'll know the terms "red pill" and "blue pill". They refer to a choice between the willingness to learn a potentially unsettling or life-changing truth, by taking the red pill, or remaining in blissful ignorance with the blue pill.

This book contains some red pills, which could change your life. If you're up for that.

Blue pills aren't worth bothering about. So we won't.

Here goes …

1

JUMPING RIGHT IN

I once read a brilliant book by a bloke called Donald Miller which included a story about a man who spent his time teaching disadvantaged youths to play chess. His reasoning was simple: to win a chess match, you need to make *a succession of good decisions*. One or two brilliant decisions in a string of poor ones just won't cut it. You need to make good decisions *consistently* if you want to win at chess.

Life is much the same, the more consistently you make good decisions, the better your outcomes are likely to be.

——— **"** ———

I am not a product of my circumstances.
I am a product of my decisions.

—STEPHEN COVEY

Now of course, some life decisions are easy—you don't need to be a rocket scientist to know that drinking and driving will eventually end in tears. But not all decisions are that obvious. Often you just don't know what a good decision would be in a given situation. Should you prioritise payments into your home loan, or should you prioritise them into your retirement fund? Should you leave your day job and start your own business? Should you date this person or run for the hills?

With questions such as these, and many, many others, you can't always trust your emotions or your gut. You *want* to make good decisions. You try to consider all the pros and cons, you even ask Google and ChatGPT. But without some level of *direct knowledge* or *prior experience* you just can't be sure that the course of action you choose is going to turn out well.

This is where wise mentors, wise parents, wise spouses and some common sense are invaluable. As is about 1000 years of actual life experience.

Unfortunately, I only have about 55 years of life experience plus an odd assortment of received wisdom which managed to sneak past my ego and hang around in my head long enough to get noticed. Nevertheless, maybe you can find in these pages some useful stuff which I wish I'd learned a bit earlier, and maybe it'll save you a few tears of life experience and even the odd wrong turn. Oh, and by the way,

―――― 66 ――――

"For what it's worth: it's never too late … to be whoever you want to be. There's no time limit. Start whenever you want. You can change. Or stay the same. There are no rules to this thing. You can make the best or the worst of it. I hope you make the best of it. I hope you see things that startle you. I hope you feel things you never felt before. I hope you meet people with a different point of view. I hope you live a life you're proud of. And if you find that you're not, I hope you have the strength to start all over again."

―BENJAMIN BUTTON, THE CURIOUS CASE OF BENJAMIN BUTTON

READ THIS …

To Own a Dragon: Reflections on Growing Up Without a Father by Donald Miller and John MacMurray. This is an inspiring read for anyone who didn't grow up with a good father. And for everyone who wants to be one.

2

WHO YOU ARE

You probably don't remember this but there was a time when you were a world-class athlete. An incredible, stupendous winner. You beat more competitors in a single, desperate, winner-takes-all race for survival than the greatest athletes in the history of the Olympics ever beat in their entire lives. *You* out-lasted, out-swam and out-muscled about 500 million sperm competitors to secure a prize which will determine the very existence of countless future generations. Just imagine. You're a beast! A machine! Well done! Incredible!

And it gets better. Not only did you have to get there at the front of the queue, but you had to be *accepted* by the (very discerning) egg before you were allowed in. The egg had the final say as to which sperm-cell fertilised it. So not only did you reach the egg at the front of the queue, but the egg also deemed *you* to be worthy of *your life* AND of the lives of *countless future generations*. My word! Think of that!

And so here we are today, a few years later. I'm not sure how you feel about that epic victory now. Or how worthy you feel right now. Maybe life has dulled your shine a bit. Maybe you've lost your way a bit. Or maybe you're powering on and up, eager for the next great challenge.

No matter. I just wanted to remind you that there was a time when you were a great winner. And absolutely worthy of hope and a future.

And that is still who you are. So, keep going and read on.

#YoureAWinner #YoureWorthy

3

HOW TO NOT WASTE YOUR LIFE

Our time on this earth is limited. For sure, when I was twenty, I thought I was immortal and could walk on water. I also knew a lot about everything! But gradually I began to suspect that possibly none of these was completely true and that I should probably endeavour to *do* something and *be* someone and *live* a bit more intentionally; or this thing called "life" might just pass by, barely lived.

—— **"** ——

"I went to the woods because I wanted to live deliberately.
I wanted to live deep and suck out all the marrow
of life. To put to rout all that was not life; and not,
when I came to die, discover that I had not lived."

—N.H. KLEINBAUM, DEAD POETS SOCIETY

I can remember some ancient philosophers (aka Speakers at my high school assembly) waggling their fingers at us boys, staring over their spectacles and admonishing gravely "life is short, don't waste it!".

Whaaat? How do you not *waste* your life!? Great, another thing to worry about!

Luckily over the succeeding years I've come to realise two things; firstly, for most of us life is not actually that short. And anyway, you've got very little control over the length of your life. So, no point in stressing too much on that score. Secondly, the secret behind not "wasting" one's life is to simply understand that you can either *spend* time or *invest* time.

Invested time results in *compounding benefits*. It includes things like

- Reading (quality stuff)
- Travel
- Exercise
- Mindfulness
- Appreciating music and art
- Honing a skill
- Building relationships
- Raising children (well)

Spent time has no compounding benefits. It includes things like

- Scrolling through inane videos on social media,
- Watching TV alone (as opposed to watching with someone significant and making it a bonding time. For example, sport with friends, or movies with your squeeze),
- Worrying (as opposed to working out a solution, which turns time *spent* worrying into time *invested* in progressing),
- Having an argument (which leads to anger, as opposed to having a discussion which leads to understanding and progress towards resolution),
- Nursing a grudge or resentment,
- Trying to live someone else's life, or the life someone else expects you to live.

When choosing what to do with your spare moments, prioritise *investing* time, not *spending* it. That's it. **Just be intentional**. If you can do that, you won't be wasting your life.

Good stuff. Next …

#InvestTime #LiveYourOwnLife #BeMindful

4

SOME BALLS BOUNCE

Now hang on a sec you say: "It's all very well to say I should choose *investing* time over *spending* it. Easy to say. But do you have any idea just how hectic my life is!? I don't *get* to choose. I'm running flat out just to survive. Choose?! I wish I could choose!!"

I hear you: It doesn't seem to matter whether you're cramming for the next test, or juggling family with career with homemaking, or fighting to keep bills paid and children educated and career growing and being responsible etc etc etc. Life is truly hectic. And it all seems to be getting faster and faster. With more demands and more expectations from everyone and everything. I know. It's freakin' exhausting.

I can distinctly remember my thirties—I was a husband and a dad of three small squeakers, trying to plough a furrow in the corporate world and desperately trying to hold it all together. In truth I felt like the g-string on my old guitar, with everything just winding me tighter and tighter. It seemed relentless. My mental pitch kept getting higher and tighter and more stressed and more exhausted. I lost my sense of humour, I barked at the kids and snapped at the wife. Sooner or later, I felt, something was going to snap with a loud, high-pitched twang!

Well firstly, if you feel like this, then let me encourage you: you are tougher than you think (see the next chapter).

Secondly, you're not alone. Believe me, almost everyone around you feels the same way at different times. And thirdly, there is a way through. Keep calm and read on … ☺

One of the legendary stories about dealing with the demands and priorities of life is the *5-Balls-of-Life Speech* by Coca-Cola's former CEO Brian Dyson[1]. He said:

———— 66 ————

"[…] Imagine life as a game in which you are juggling some five balls in the air. You name them work, family, health, friends and spirit. And you're keeping all of these in the air. You will soon understand that work is a rubber ball. If you drop it, it will bounce back. But the other four balls—family, health, friends and spirit—are made of glass. If you drop one of these, they will be irrevocably scuffed, marked, nicked, damaged or even shattered. They will never be the same. You must understand that and strive for balance in your life".

Excellent advice. But, in my personal experience, implementation wasn't always so easy. There were times when I felt I had a lot more than five balls in the air, and to make matters worse the damn things kept morphing into different versions with new demands!

The pressures of work, family, health, studies, finances, friends and spirituality were often in competition. So where to begin? And what to prioritise?

Over time I began to realise that being intentional is fundamental to finding balance. *Busyness is your enemy*. Read that again.

> Busyness is the enemy of family, health, friends, spirituality, and quality of life.

With a non-stop busy schedule, you're on the road to burn-out. Excessive busyness has a directly negative effect on your well-being,

---

1   172nd Commencement of the Georgia Tech Institute, 6 Sept 1991. Brian Dyson.

relationships and mental peace. It robs you of space to *think*.

Instead, *seek to simplify your life*. And be serious about it. Be ruthless about removing the stuff that keeps you manically busy but adds little value or enjoyment. Maybe start by thinking deeply about the difference between when something needs to be perfect and when good enough is, well, good enough.

I'm starting to learn that many of the balls I'm trying so desperately to juggle *are* made of rubber. And in fact, some balls wouldn't even be missed if I dropped them and never picked them up again! Other balls are imaginary—just me trying to meet the weight of expectations that others place on me. And sometimes even those expectations are all in my own head. They don't actually exist! Does my spouse/boss/child/parent *really* expect me to be perfect in everything, all the time? Probably not. That's probably in my own head. It's me placing unrealistic burdens on myself.

On the other hand, if they do expect me to be perfect in everything all the time, then they're going to have to swallow a Red Pill—I'm not perfect. And neither are they. Let's all learn to live with it and carry on.

That said, there *are* a lot of very real, very important balls. And the challenge is how to tell the difference between balls that are made of glass and those that are made of rubber or are imaginary.

How to recognise your balls

Here are some questions that may help you to distinguish between rubber and glass balls. Ask yourself …

What's the long-term impact of this ball?

This question goes straight to the point of how much this ball you're juggling really matters. Remember, this question applies to ALL the balls you're juggling, not just your work-related balls. For most people, family, health and well-being should matter as much or more than work.

Another perspective on the long-term impact question is to ask a slightly different question: Will this matter a week from now, a month from now, a year from now, ten years from now?

> In short, prioritise what is important. What is important is much more important than what is urgent. Read this last sentence again.

Who else depends on this ball?

This question places each ball in a human context. The ball may or may not be critical to you, but how critical is it to others? Your spouse, your children, your parents, your boss, your colleagues, your friends? Red Pill: you can't always do what you want to do when you want to do it. Welcome to adulting—you have some responsibilities to others as well.

Of course, you shouldn't let your decision-making be driven solely by other people's needs, but you do need to consider them. Especially those that you care about or on whom you rely or in whom you're investing for the long term.

That said, beware taking on responsibility for stuff which others are conveniently pushing onto you just because they know you can't say no.

——— 66 ———

"Let today mark a new beginning for you. Give yourself permission to say NO without feeling guilty, mean or selfish. Anybody who gets upset and/or expects you to say YES all of the time clearly doesn't have your best interests at heart. Always remember: You have a right to say NO without having to explain yourself. Be at peace with your decisions."

—STEPHANIE LAHART

What actual value does this ball add to me and to those I love?
When you're juggling a lot of balls, it's easy to start looking at all of them as equal burdens. That's usually not the case. One way to differentiate between the ones that are more or less important is to consider the relative value they add to your life. Which balls add more value (and remember value includes well-being), and which add less? What are the good things that result from keeping this particular ball in the air? Considering the relative value-add of each ball helps you to prioritize the balls you're juggling.

What if I dropped this ball, could I (we) recover?
Stop for a moment and think about the setbacks you've had in your life which you've recovered from. Many of those setbacks were probably so minor that you quickly forgot about them and moved on. A few were more serious and took longer to recover from. But you did, maybe with a few scars to show you survived and a few life-lessons learned. There may even be some that smacked you so hard that you're still struggling to recover—a divorce, a nervous breakdown, a bankruptcy. But hopefully those smackdowns have been very, very few. The point is this: most setbacks are recoverable, and reasonably quickly (say within a few months). Which means, of course, that most balls are rubber. Most balls will bounce. I hope that takes the pressure off a bit.

Can I get some help with this ball?
Don't drop important balls because you're out of your depth or exhausted or demoralised. Talk to your network. Generally, you'll be amazed at how keen people are to help. Of course, you don't need to take on every bit of help that is offered. On the contrary, put your own brain into gear and be discriminating about which help offered is actually likely to be helpful in reality.

It takes maturity to leverage your network for advice and insight and experience. I was too proud to do this in my twenties. Now I can't do it enough.

—————— **66** ——————

"What is the bravest thing you've ever said? asked
the boy. 'Help,' said the horse. 'Asking for help isn't
giving up,' said the horse. 'It's refusing to give up."

—CHARLIE MACKESY, THE BOY, THE MOLE, THE FOX AND THE HORSE

Should I be juggling this ball at all?

It's possible, probably likely, that you're juggling some balls that really aren't yours to juggle at all. So stop. Ask yourself the question, "Should I even be juggling this ball?" Maybe the answer is "yes", and maybe it's "yes, but not right now". Maybe the answer is someone else should be juggling it. Perhaps the answer is no one should be juggling it at all—it adds no value!

Or perhaps it's a self-levitating ball that you only need to check in on every now and then only for course corrections.

Children and work colleagues often fall into the levitating ball category: resist the urge to micro-manage their every move. They will only resent you for it, and you will probably become the person you really don't want to be. Everyone knows the maxim: *"Children don't do what you say. They do what you do"*. So your primary and most important role is to set them a worthy example. Work subordinates are just the same. Focus on holding them accountable for WHAT they achieve, rather than micro-managing HOW they achieve it. Chances are, you'll be surprised by their creativity.

Anyway, you won't know which balls to put down unless you stop to ask the question. In all likelihood, there is a very high probability that you're busting a gut juggling balls that you don't really have to.

The Complexity Curve

The point in all this is to *try to minimise the number of balls you are juggling.* The graphic below is one of my favourites: I call it the Complexity Curve.

We all intuitively understand that the greater the number of balls we're trying to juggle, the more complexity we have in our lives and the greater the stress that we will feel. What we don't always appreciate however is that it's not a straight-line relationship between the number of balls and complexity: adding an extra ball adds *exponentially* to the complexity and stress in your life. By the time you're going from 7 balls to 8 balls you're adding an *enormous* amount of complexity and stress into your life—way, way more than going from 3 to 4 balls.

The good news is that if you remove the 8th ball and go back to 7, you reverse down the same curve and by so doing you *remove* an enormous amount of complexity and stress from your life. Cool huh!

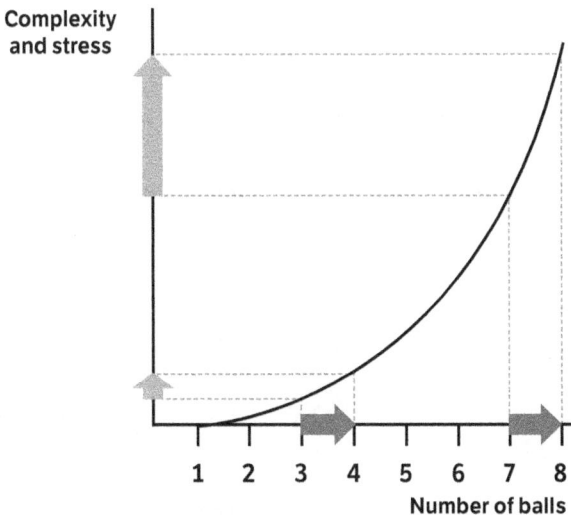

Figure 1: The Complexity Curve

> **To me this is one of the golden rules of a balanced life:**
> Be ruthless about minimising the number of balls you have in
> the air at any one time. And then, be sure to know which of the
> remaining ones are glass.

A little happiness goes a long way

Think about what gives you joy. Do that stuff as much as possible.
Be intentional about building activities into your schedule that are
important to you. Spend some time *every week* doing something that
you enjoy. This could be playing sport or helping at a charity or entertaining friends. Or, better still, a date night with your significant other.
Every week mind! Don't skimp on this.

Try to get away into nature—a weekend in the bush or mountains or
even a day in the park will rejuvenate you like you can't believe. Especially if it's time shared with family or friends.

Steve Jobs, the founder of Apple, gave the following advice:

———— **❝** ————

*"If you live each day as if it were your last, one day you
will be right. What if, every morning, you stood in front
of the bathroom mirror and asked yourself, "if today
was my last day, would I still do what I'm going to do
today? Would I still juggle each of these balls? If the
answer to that question is "no" for too many days in a
row, then maybe something needs to change in your life."*

Maybe you need to put down some balls or ask for help. I hope you
have the courage to do that.

In short, keep your priorities straight. Taking care of your family, your
health, your relationships and your spiritual wellbeing is not selfish.
It's sustaining.

—— **66** ——

*Maybe you're stressed not because you're doing
too much. Maybe you're stressed because you're
doing too little of what makes you feel alive.*

So ACT. Action makes all the difference. Procrastination results in worry without progress. If busyness is the enemy of family, health, friends, spirituality, and quality of life, then procrastination is surely as bad.

Do this now:
1. Write a list of all the balls you're juggling.
2. Place them in order of value (importance).
3. Look at the bottom one and plan a way to put it down.
4. Repeat. As often as required.

#GlassBallsDontBounce
#Simplify
#Busyness
#OkaytoSayNo
#Rest

Businesses have balls too

This principle of *simplifying* is equally applicable to business. You'll be amazed at how many businesses could dramatically improve their profitability if they sold *fewer* product types and slashed their red tape (which they generally to refer to as "admin"). The aim is to concentrate more closely on those aspects of the business that *really* add value—their glass balls.

——— 66 ———

*"80% of the results come from 20% of the causes.
A few things are important; most are not."*

—RICHARD KOCH

READ THIS ...

If you're at any level of management in a business, in my view, these are essential reads:

The 80/20 Principle: The Secret of Achieving More with Less by Richard Koch. The 80/20 principle is one of the great secrets of highly effective people and organizations. Koch shows how you can achieve much more with much less effort, time, and resources, simply by identifying and focusing your efforts on the 20 percent that really counts.

Simplify: How the Best Businesses in the World Succeed by Richard Koch and Greg Lockwood. This book takes the 80/20 Principle to the next level. It's rocket fuel for any business.

#8020Principle

5

YOU'RE TOUGHER THAN YOU THINK

Remember Chapter 2 when I reminded you that you were once the world's greatest champion? And that is still who you are? Imagine if you could remember what it took to win that race against 500 million competitors. It must have been excruciatingly exhausting. Not a moment of respite, the gun went off and you fought your way to the front, and you kept on going. You ignored the tail cramps and the fatigue and the buffeting of competitors. You shut out every thought and emotion and pain that didn't propel you forward. And ultimately, despite the odds, you won. Epic!

Since then, sweet victories in the races of life might not have been quite as regular or as epic. But take heart, in most of life it's not the winning of an individual race that really matters, it's cultivating a *winning mindset*.

The US Navy Seals, the best-of-the-best amongst the world's elite special forces, have something called the **40 Percent Rule**. It's simply this:

> When your mind tells you that you're exhausted, fried, totally tapped out, you're really only 40 percent done. You still have 60 percent left in your tank.

Well, that's cool for them isn't it. Very motivating I'm sure. But at the same time very depressing for the rest of us—not many ordinary (viz real) people can get to the point of exhaustion and then push through even more of the same based purely on willpower.

The truth is, neither can the Navy Seals. Instead, they have a technique which, when combined with willpower, enables them to push through endurance barriers that seem impossible.

Paraphrasing **Jeff Haden** in his online article (see *Read This* panel at end of chapter):

Imagine I put you on an exercise bike and ask you to pedal as hard as you can for five seconds so we can measure the power you generate. You give it everything and pump out the power. After five seconds you're breathing harder and your heart rate is up, but you're maintaining.

Then, after a short break, I ask you to ride hard again, but this time to just keep going for as long as you can so we can measure your endurance.

If you're more or less average, you'll last about 12 minutes on the endurance test before you give up, totally knackered.

But then I ask you to immediately repeat the five second, power test. You're crazy, you think. You're already totally empty. Pedal more? Impossible. You stopped precisely because you can't pedal any more.

But it turns out you can: If you're like the average person, you can produce three times more power in the burst than you did during the endurance test.

So why did you give up because you couldn't pedal any more ... yet somehow crank out substantial power seconds later in a short burst? Clearly you weren't as exhausted as you thought you were.

So why did you stop? In part, the problem lies in your head: It's very hard to keep going *indefinitely* when your heart is pounding, and your legs are burning, *and* you don't know how long the pain is going to last. That's physically *and mentally* draining—a combination which makes it almost impossible to keep pushing past what you think is your limit.

For most of us *"keep going for as long as you can"* is just too open ended. It feels endless and pointless. If *"for as long as you can"* is the goal, then what's the difference between 5 minutes or 10 minutes or 30 minutes? When the pain becomes too much, we might as well stop.

It turns out that to keep going, most of us need a finish line, a *finite* goal, a defined end to the pain. Then, even when we feel exhausted, cranking out another five seconds is (relatively) nothing.

The same can be true of many things in life. Some challenges seem to last forever: maybe you're struggling at work, or in your marriage, or with illness, or with child rearing, or trying to stay sober, or just trying to lose weight. When we're battling with difficult, long-term challenges sooner or later we are all tempted to walk away, to just give up. We do it because we feel empty and demoralised and just plain exhausted, and we're convinced that we have no more to give.

Usually however, we can push *just a little bit more* and keep going for just a little bit longer. But very rarely can we keep going *indefinitely*.

So let's take a leaf from the Navy Seals: try this …

Turn 'as long as you can' … into 'five second' bursts

Take launching a new business as an example. It's tough! Bootstrapping your way through a constant—seemingly endless—series of challenges and setbacks, and difficult decisions, and long nights and longer weekends, doesn't just require physical effort. The mental endurance required is extreme—especially since you have no idea when you will finally turn the corner and the struggle will, if not end, at least ease off a bit.

That's why so many entrepreneurs quit. When today is hard, and you know tomorrow will be hard, and you have no idea how many more tomorrows you will ultimately have to endure, it's incredibly hard to keep going even though you apparently still have 60 percent remaining in your stay-the-course tank.

So what can you do? Turn "as long as you can" into your own version of "five second" bursts.

As Jeff Haden advises: Instead of thinking in terms of an endless number of tasks stretching over the horizon into the future, set a finite target for each day. Cap it at five. Or ten. Or two. Whatever your execution plan calls for. That way you'll take your mind off tomorrow, and focus fully on today, and on doing each task to the best of your ability. *And* you'll have the positive reinforcement of a task completed. Then take a small breather before you tackle the next burst.

When "for as long as you can" is the time window, it's natural to lose motivation and to focus on the effort rather than the task. And to give up.

But when "all" you have to do is do the best you can *for today*, or for this *one task*, then it's much easier to find the energy and the focus that will get you to the finish line.

I can't say I've mastered this in my own life yet. But I'm trying. And that's my task for today.

READ THIS ...

This chapter is based on a concept popularized by Navy Seal Dave Goggins in Jesse Itzler's book *Living With a Seal*.

And the online article: *https://incafrica.com/article/ jeff-haden-success-persistence-seal-40-percent- rule-high-achiever-mindset*

#FourtyPercentRule

6

WHAT MY GRAN TOLD ME

My mom's mom was a remarkable woman. She drove heavy duty trucks for the army during World War II. She outlived three husbands, one of whom was an alcoholic. She endured a time of real poverty, living in one room with her husband and a small child. She lost another child at birth. She knew what it was to be a single mom. Yet she was one of the most positive and resilient people I ever knew.

I can remember her telling me that: "*Nothing lasts forever. Nothing very good. And nothing very bad*". In other words, don't think the good times will last forever—expect change. And prepare. And similarly, when times are really tough—hang in. Grit your teeth and keep going. "*This too shall pass*".

"Easy to say" you may be thinking, but my Gran had the life scars to back-up her words. She taught me an incredible life lesson:

Try to cultivate a long-term view.

In the short-term, life can be massively volatile with joyful highs (like passing your exams or your wedding day) and crushing lows (like losing your job or being publicly humiliated on social media). But, "*this too shall pass*". Try not to react too quickly or too drastically when your emotions are very high, or very low. Give yourself some time to settle down. Sleep on it. In five or ten years, you'll probably hardly remember the crisis of today. As gran used to say, "*where there is life, there is hope*".

Granny was born in 1910, four years before the outbreak of World War I—the "war to end all wars". It resulted in about 20 million deaths and 21 million wounded. Never before had the world seen horror and devastation on such a scale. Then, when the soldiers finally returned home in 1919, they brought with them the Spanish Flu which killed another 50 million people worldwide. One fifth of the world's population contracted the virus. Within months, it had killed more people than any other illness or war in recorded history. Can you imagine the prevailing sentiment—four years of devastating war followed immediately by a global pandemic the likes of which the world had never seen. As if that wasn't enough, just as the infection rates were beginning to drop in 1920 the world fell into a crippling depression with massive unemployment and widespread economic hardship. That lasted another two years.

Many people thought the end of the world had come. Seriously. Who wouldn't have? Many turned to alcohol. Many lost hope. The suicide rate exploded. The very next year there was an armed rebellion in her home country. It was a mad, bad and dangerous time to be alive. Gran had to leave school, without finishing, to work in a shop to help feed the family.

Less than seven years later, when Gran was 19, the Wall Street Crash of 1929 wiped out personal savings and crippled economies around the world. It ushered in the Great Depression which lasted for ten years! Millions of people around the world lost their jobs and families queued at government soup kitchens to survive.

The year the Great Depression finally ended, 1939, saw the outbreak of World War II. An estimated 70–85 million people died, about 3% of the entire global population of the time. Talk about desperate times!

Gran also witnessed the progression of flight from propeller driven biplanes to supersonic jets and men walking on the moon. She lived through the cold war and the Cuban missile crisis when the world teetered on the brink of nuclear war. She lived through the global oil crisis in the 1970's and saw the emergence of rock music and the hippie culture. She saw Elvis come and go. She saw the birth of communism and the fall of the Soviet Union. She was alive during the holocaust, and she saw the formation of the State of Israel.

Figure 2: Dorothea Lange's 1936 photo is an iconic photograph of the misery of the Great Depression. *Source: Library of Congress, Prints & Photographs Division, FSA/OWI Collection*

The point I'm coming to is this: life is crazy and unpredictable and terrifying and awesome and wonderful. Some of it you will have some level of control over, but over much of it, none at all. So, try to take a longer-term view. When things are dark and terrifying and apparently without hope—go speak to an old person. Chances are that they will be able to tell you from personal life experience—*"this too shall pass"*. In five- or ten-years' time, you will probably hardly remember this current crisis. So, try to keep it in perspective, a longer-term perspective, and *keep going*.

For many people, me included, a longer-term perspective includes an *eternal* perspective. What I mean by that is this: without something greater than yourself to give it all meaning, life can be really tough and disturbing and even rather pointless. But I strongly believe that there *is* a bigger picture, a greater purpose for each of us. Something that brings meaning to our lives and experiences. More on that later.

In the meantime, you will likely find that in many areas of life—your marriage, your job, your finances, piano lessons, your health, whatever; sometimes you just need to "*Keep Calm and KBO*".

That's life. Keep going. Take a longer-term view. And KBO. I'm sure your Gran would agree.

Figure 3: Churchill's famous encouragement was delivered equally to the highest generals and the lowest soldiers during Britain's darkest days in World War II (abbreviated to "KBO" when in polite company). *Source: https://tybennett.com*

#TakeALongTermView
#KBO

7

DON'T IGNORE RED FLAGS

R ed Flags refer to early warning signals of risk or danger. When I was in the army, Red Flags were placed at all the access points to a shooting-range whenever live firing was underway. It was best not to ignore them.

But you'll be amazed at how often people ignore Red Flags in their own lives, in their careers, in their health, in their finances and in their relationships. And then can't understand why things go a bit pear shaped.

As a child it somehow felt wrong to dwell too much on negative stuff. I was taught to "count my blessings" and "be grateful for what you have" and "be positive" and "believe the best of everyone". I'm truly grateful for those lessons. I believe in them strongly and I know they're good and true.

Unfortunately, I think I might have zoned out when my parents taught me the balancing lesson: "don't ignore Red Flags". As a result, at times I've ignored flags that demarcated live firing on the range. I've convinced myself that the flag was just a normal part of life rather than a warning signal. And so, I've done nothing and blundered on.

However, as I slowly gathered a bit more life experience, I started realising the incredible value of Red Flag awareness in almost every facet of life, from relationships to business, to mental and physical health. Now I try to incorporate awareness of Red Flags into my life in a positive way.

For instance, I've come to realise that the *culture* in any organisation is fundamentally important in determining the progress or decline of that organisation. Be it in a business or in a family or in a sports team: where there is mutual respect and personal integrity and positive intent, everyone benefits. But where there is toxicity, or selfishness, or negative intent, everyone suffers. And eventually things fall apart.

I'm really very serious about this. I think it's foundational to leadership at any level in any context.

When I was running a business some years ago, one of the core values which we tried to uphold was to "*at all times act with positive intent*". This value didn't prevent us from having difficult or robust conversations, but we only ever had those with positive intentions for the individual and for the organisation. I simply did not tolerate people acting with negative intent, you know, the malicious gossipers, the underminers, the bullies. In fact, we confronted the perpetrators of negative intent head on. And if the individual refused (or didn't have the character) to change and start acting with positive intent, we showed them the door. Negative intent is a major character Red Flag for me. It's destructive and it shouldn't be tolerated, either in ourselves or in others. Not anywhere.

STORY #1

How to kill a wolf

According to tradition, this is how an Inuit hunter kills a wolf ...

First, the hunter kills a seal. Then he dips his knife in the seals blood and allows the blood to freeze on his blade. He does this again and again, coating the razor-sharp blade of his hunting knife in seal blood and allowing it to freeze in the arctic air. He adds layer after layer of blood until the blade is completely concealed by the frozen blood.

Then, the hunter plunges the hilt of his knife into the snow and tamps it fast—the blood covered blade standing up in air.

Eventually a wolf will pick up the scent of the blood on the icy air and, following his nose, will come to investigate. He finds the knife and sniffs it suspiciously. He's hungry, he's starving. He smells the blood. He's cautious. Way back in the recesses of his brain a red flag is waving. But he smells the blood. And he's hungry. So he takes a tentative lick. It's good. And nothing bad happens.

So, he has another lick. And then another. The red flag seems to have disappeared—great, a false alarm. He begins to lick faster and faster, more and more vigorously. It's bitterly cold, his tongue is slightly numb, but he can taste the blood. And it's so, so good. He wants more and more. He can't help himself.

Feverishly now, all caution abandoned, the wolf licks the frozen blood. His craving is so great that he does not notice as the blade slowly becomes exposed. He doesn't realise when his lust for blood is being satisfied not by the blood of the seal but by his own, as his tongue is slowly cut to ribbons.

He continues to crave more and more until, eventually, inevitably the wolf dies from the loss of his own blood.

And so it is with many of the dangers in this world—they seem small and insignificant at first, so you ignore the Red Flags. Or, by the time you realise the danger, you're in too deep, or too committed, you feel trapped. Please, don't be lulled into ignoring red flags. Run away and live another day.

And if you do feel that you're in too deep, you're too committed, trapped, then *get help*. You need wise counsel from people who truly love you. Or trained professionals. And you need to put your own brain into gear as well. Take ownership. And act! Here are a few common red flags to watch out for:

Anger

Righteous, controlled anger at injustice or wrongdoing is admirable.

But someone displaying selfish anger, or a temper is to be treated with serious caution. Of course, we all have our limits and sometimes we snap. BUT any form of violence toward you, loved ones, strangers, and even animals is a serious Red Flag. Don't ignore this one. Anger patterns are usually a deep-seated character issue. They don't just go away.

And let me be clear, I'm not just talking about men who physically abuse women or bully those who are weaker. I'm including verbal attacks that demean and humiliate. I've seen women do this to their men. I've seen mothers do this to their children. Stop it. It's super destructive. Do not provoke anger or bitterness or resentment in others.

Our role as mature adults is ALWAYS to act with positive intent. My role as a husband and father is to encourage my wife and children to blossom into the fullness of who they were created to be. To build them up, not to break them down. To build their confidence and their self-esteem. To encourage them to do more and be more, not to intimidate them or belittle them or force them into my mould.

And my role as a business leader, or a community leader is exactly the same.

If you or someone you are close to has anger issues, or has a mean streak or is a manipulator, or is over-controlling, or is a gossiper or commonly exhibits bad intent then recognise these as Red Flags. Walk away. Or get proper, professional help.

Conflict Avoidance

The opposite side of anger is conflict avoidance—the slow puncture of many a relationship.

THE FIRST RULE OF PASSIVE AGGRESSIVE CLUB IS... YOU KNOW WHAT? NEVER MIND, **IT'S FINE.**

Relationships that cannot handle conflict in a respectful and constructive way run the risk of developing smouldering resentment and passive aggression. As uncomfortable as it may be, embracing constructive conflict and politely worded disagreement is a crucial element of all relationships.

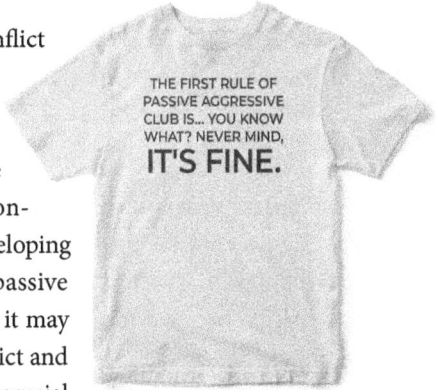

This is true in the home and in the workplace. Without the willingness and skills to deal with conflict in a productive and respectful manner *with positive intent,* serious matters can never be resolved. And one party will always feel unheard and degraded.

If you or someone you are close to continually avoids conflict, then that's a Red Flag.

And it may require a bit of introspection: if someone continually avoids conflict with me, could that actually be *my* issue and not theirs? Do *I* make it difficult for people to raise issues with me because I'm too defensive or volatile or dismissive? Hmmm. Something to think about. How can I be more approachable?

Lack of emotional intelligence

Emotional Intelligence (or maturity) is the ability to recognise, understand and manage how we think, feel and act. Also referred to as "emotional quotient" or "EQ", emotional intelligence is super essential to *every* aspect of life that I can think of.

In my early career as an engineer, I thought that the way to succeed was to apply high levels of technical professionalism, a drive to get the task done to the highest level of perfection as efficiently as possible. Sounds right. Yet as I've gotten older and more experienced and maybe matured a bit myself, I've come to realise that all those things are only a part of what is really required. And in fact quite a small (albeit important) part.

The biggest and most important determinant of overall success in business and in life in general, is the ability to manage your own psychology in a given situation. And the skillset to respond to the psychology of others in a mature and constructive way.

This is especially true when you're under stress—like in a difficult working environment, or you're not sleeping, or things aren't good in your personal relationships. Low EQ in either yourself or in others is a major Red Flag. Have your radar up on this one, and don't ignore it. Being married to a low EQ person will wither you. They will drain your joy and your self-confidence. Make sure you are truly okay with a partner's EQ before you tie yourself to them. Don't "settle" on this one.

Do everything you can to develop your own EQ. But don't imagine that your high EQ will compensate for a partner's low EQ. It won't. Red pill.

READ THIS ...

Emotional Intelligence: Why It Can Matter More Than IQ by Daniel Goleman. EQ includes self-awareness and impulse control, persistence, zeal, and self-motivation, empathy and social deftness. Far more than IQ, these are the qualities that mark people who excel in life, whose relationships flourish, who are stars in the workplace.

Emotional Intelligence 2.0 by Travis Bradberry and Jean Greaves. Knowing what EQ is and knowing how to use it to improve your life are two very different things. This book delivers a step-by-step program for building your EQ to enable you to achieve your fullest potential.

And the same is true in the workplace. I once worked for a multi-national company where the CEO was an extremely dominant and aggressive individual. Behind his back people would joke that his mantra was "*Be reasonable. Do it my way.*" I can remember sitting in executive meetings where the first thing anyone would say when addressing him was "I agree with you". Everyone was too terrified to put forward a different perspective for fear that he would humiliate them or that it would damage their careers. He'd effectively crippled the minds of his leadership team and gutted their independent thinking.

It was a toxic culture which, unfortunately, soon started to be mimicked further down the organisation. It was disastrous for morale. And terrible for long-term business performance. I lasted two years. And within another 18 months the share price had halved.

——— 66 ———

"CEOs are hired for their intellect and business expertise—
and fired for a lack of emotional intelligence."

—DANIEL GOLEMAN

You can't always choose who your boss is. But you can choose how long you stay. Don't stay in an environment that is debilitating and wearisome for so long that you get conditioned into thinking that this is "just how things are" (or worse, you start mimicking bad EQ culture). Instead, stay only long enough to witness the good and bad outcomes of good and bad EQ. Look, listen and learn. At the very least, experiencing bad EQ for a while will toughen you mentally. But hopefully it will also inform how you want to (and don't want to) behave.

Here are some **classic signs of people with low emotional intelligence** (you'll notice that these people are mostly focused on themselves).

- They always have to be 'right'.
- They're oblivious to other people's feelings.

- They behave insensitively or inappropriately.
- They blame others for their problems.
- They have poor coping skills.
- They have emotional outbursts.
- They struggle with relationships.
- They turn conversations toward themselves.
- They can't "read the room" so they say things that are inappropriate for the moment, or in a way that is inappropriate.

And some **signs of high EQ**:

- They cope well with change.
- They are aware of their strengths and their weaknesses. And they leverage the former for good and remedy the latter.
- They show empathy toward others.
- They pursue progress, not perfection.
- They have balanced lives.
- They're curious and eager to learn, acknowledging that they have a lot to learn.
- They express themselves assertively but politely.
- They're receptive to feedback even if it's critical.
- They praise and thank others.
- They stop and think before responding (especially in highly charged situations).
- They apologise. They forgive and forget.

Emotional intelligence is super important in determining the trajectory of your life. And the good news is that it can be learned. So be serious about it and read up. You won't regret it.

Lying

Lying isn't okay. Lying is a major red flag. I can't stress this enough. Let's be clear from the very beginning: if someone lies about small things, they will very likely lie about big things too. The reason for this is that lying very easily becomes a habit—every time you get away with it, it reinforces itself.

If someone has a mindset to deceive, it can only ever lead to tears. Trust is a fragile thing and once someone has broken it, it's a very difficult thing to rebuild.

This is true in the home, amongst friends and in business. You should set the ground rules for that—if you catch someone in a lie, even a small one, you need to be clear to them there and then that it's unacceptable and that deceit and deception can have no place in your relationship.

I would discipline my children, not always for the bad thing they had done, but always if they lied about it. I did the same at work. Sometimes things go wrong. People make mistakes. We all know that. I tried very hard to develop a culture where people realised that telling the truth, the whole truth and nothing but the truth, as soon as possible, was ALWAYS far better than being caught in deception later.

Lying is the kiss of death to trust relationships. And to credibility. And to careers.

RELATIONSHIP TIP:

Always try to avoid labelling someone too quickly. So, for instance, if you catch your child in a lie, it's far better to say "Don't lie. You're not a liar.", than to say, "You're a liar".

The first approach identifies them as an honest person who has made a mistake which can be rectified. The second, labels them negatively and leaves very little room for redemption because only YOU have the power to re-label them.

Far better to label someone in a positive way (even while calling them out for something negative), than to label them negatively and so diminish their hope of restoration.

Mismatched Worldviews or Aspirations

As with conflict avoidance, these are "slow puncture" Red Flags in most intimate relationships. They're not all deal breakers but you should recognise that they could cause serious issues in the long-term unless both parties have the maturity and enough *EQ* to deal with them or live with them.

For instance, if your partner says that they're not interested in marriage and that's something you desire, then believe them. And make a choice.

If you're a spiritual person and your partner mocks spirituality, then I'm afraid heartache lies ahead of you. It's also going to be tough if your political views are miles apart. Or if you like socializing with friends but he's a loner. Do you want a nice house in the suburbs with a dog and a goldfish, but she wants to seek enlightenment in Tibet?

Misaligned views might include where you want to live, whether you want to have children, and how you plan to tackle finances. Don't ignore these flags. They may seem small enough now but they could be the slow-burning fuses of resentment and bitterness over the horizon. Those of us who've been lucky enough to be married for a long time know that sooner or later you're going to have to fight *together* (with positive intent) for the marriage to survive. You're going to have to agree to go to counselling *together* or agree together to let go of some dreams or aspirations or change some behaviours. If only one person cares enough about marriage to fight for it in this way, then they have only one choice: to completely subjugate themselves to every whim and preference and opinion of the non-carer, to die inside and live solely to please the other, with little hope of reciprocation. I'm not sure that that classifies as a marriage.

In the long run, both parties need to find true, deep peace around misaligned worldviews or aspirations, and be willing to compromise. If not, that Red Flag just got a whole lot bigger and a whole lot closer. Achtung!

No Friends or outside interests

For most of us, family and friends provide an important sense of community. It's a major Red Flag if someone in your life is negatively affecting your relationship with those you love, especially family. Healthy relationships should never come at the cost of other healthy relationships.

Undeniably, when you or your partner doesn't have other relationships, hobbies, or goals, that is a recipe for an unhealthy, unfulfilling relationship. And by hobbies, I don't mean watching endless YouTube videos or being addicted to social media—those are Red Flags in themselves.

On the other hand, when each party has its own sense of self, you can enrich each other and your bond. If someone relies on you entirely and always for their sense of happiness and entertainment, that can lead to feelings of suffocation, resentment, and unhappiness. Red flag!

Persistent Jealousy or Distrust

Another common Red Flag is jealousy and distrust. Trust is a crucial part of any healthy relationship. A major sign of an unstable relationship is when partners, friends, colleagues, or family members distrust one another.

Now there are two sides to this trust equation: Firstly, you should *never give the other person cause to distrust you*. Instead, you should endeavour to live a life which is "blameless and innocent, above reproach."[2] And so should the other party. If either of you ignores this, then distrust will naturally and inevitably follow. Here's a simple example: when you're in an exclusive relationship with someone, like dating or marriage, you can't have one-on-one lunches or coffees or visits with anyone from the opposite sex who isn't related to you. Even if it's totally innocent in your mind, you need to consider what impression

---

2   Philippians 2:15

it might create in someone else's mind, either your significant other or anyone else who might see you. This is a serious one, don't do stuff that could give anyone else grounds for distrust. Just don't.

The other side is when one party persistently distrusts the other even when there is no cause. Red flag! Groundless jealousy and distrust often go hand-in-hand with a desire to control who you see, who you talk to and where you go, even what you wear. Red flags!

Of course, we all have doubts sometimes. But healthy relationships require trust on both sides.

So what erodes trust?

- **Infidelity.** If your partner has a history of infidelity in other relationships, major Red Flag.
- **Lying.** Especially about your other relationships or money.
- **Indiscretion**. If you betray confidences.

Don't mess with other people's hearts. And don't let them mess with yours. Remember the story about juggling balls in Chapter 4? In relationships, trust is a glass ball.

Substances

I enjoy a few drinks as much as the next guy and I have no problem with responsible drinking in a social setting. But drinking too often or too much is a major Red Flag. If you or your friends or your significant other get too loud, or rude, or aggressive, or mean, or flirty on the back of a few glasses, then that's a Red Flag. If having a bit too much is a common occurrence, then that's a problem. It's time to change something.

Over the long-term, the irresponsible use of alcohol is a path that leads *only* downwards. There is no upside. Only pain. You know this. So, take it seriously.

Drugs are even worse. Don't lie to yourself, it's not funny or cool to use recreational drugs, even occasionally. It's stupid. You know this.

Experimenting with drugs *will* lead on to bigger drugs, which *will* destroy your life and those that love you, and ultimately they *will* kill you. And don't give me that rubbish about "oh, it's only occasionally at a party", or "it's only when I need to destress". Bulldust. You're delusional. I know enough people who've fried their brains through drugs and become seriously sad problems to themselves and everyone around them. Open your eyes next time you drive downtown: drugs and homelessness and prostitution and violence and crime and loneliness go together.

If you thought the story of the wolf in Story #1 was cool but mythical. Here's a real-life version …

The Unravelling

Some years ago, a work colleague confided in me the road that his family had walked after drugs got hold of his only daughter, Beth. It started, as it so often does, at a party in a club. Beth was having a grand old time with her student friends. The music was pumping. The cocktails were flowing. Everything was fun fun fun. Pretty soon a friend lit up a "smoke". And soon it was offered around, and everyone had a few puffs and it was great. And everyone was laughing and happy and having fun. It made Beth feel happy too, and mellow and funny and cool. She loved it.

Naturally, a few days later she thought she'd just ask the friend if he had any more. Just for a bit of fun you understand. Or for when she just needed to chill a bit.

Of course, the friend obliged. He was so cool and he wanted her to be happy too. So he gave her a little weed and showed her how to roll her own. Super cool. And when she ran out, he fixed her up with some more. And then again. She felt like he was the only one who truly understood her. And didn't judge her. And she was falling in love. And it was wonderful. She felt so happy and so free.

One day Beth was chilling with her now boyfriend, and they smoked a little one just for the peace of it. And after a while he suggested that she try one of these little pills. It was completely harmless, and he would have one too and it would be great. So she did.

To cut a long story short, it wasn't six months and my work colleague and his wife started noticing a bit of a change in Beth. She seemed to be withdrawing from them, and to be quite moody. Then they seemed to imagine that the money in their wallets wasn't as much as they thought it had been. Then it got more clearly noticeable. And other things seemed to be missing from the house too.

Finally, they began to suspect, and they confronted Beth. Of course, she denied it. Denied any drug taking, denied knowing anything about any missing cash or anything else. They backed off. But soon enough the red flags returned and began to intensify. Finally, after a tearful confrontation, they forced their daughter to take a drugs test. Positive. They sent her for counselling. And so began the looping of counselling, promising, trying, falling, deeper than before, confronting, crying, counselling, lying, rehab, promising, trying, falling, deeper than before, stealing, lying, missing, dropped out of university, found living with the boyfriend, falling, deeper than before, stealing, missing, lying. Missing, Missing.

Very late one night my colleague got a call from some Nigerian drug dealers—they had his daughter at the window of a grimy high-rise apartment in Hillbrow—a rough, rough neighborhood in downtown Johannesburg. They had taken everything she had, including her body, in payment for the drug money she owed them. But it still wasn't enough. So now they were going to throw her out of the window unless her father came to fetch her, with a bag full of cash.

Of course he went. But when he came back home, he was a broken man.

And her life was shattered. There is no return to normal after you live through what she had lived through. Beth was diseased physically and mentally. And it wasn't the end.

Outside of a miracle, there is no happy ending.

No happy marriage, no happy family, no successful career ever included drugs. EVER. Believe it. This is a very RED pill. Substance abuse is serious. If you or someone you know is struggling, you need to wake-up and get professional help. Now. Today.

I'm an addict too.

I was chatting to a friend of mine recently, and he said an interesting thing to me: "*at some level, all of us are addicted to something. For some it may be alcohol or drugs, but for others it's the dopamine hit that comes from shopping, or porn, or gambling, or social media, or power, even food*". And then he related his personal story of the trauma that porn had wrought in his marriage. It was an incredible story of a good man who had gotten trapped, and a wife who had been devastated. But more importantly of how they had navigated their way through it *together*.

Then he told me that he knew that he was still an addict and always would be, but that he had been "sober" for five years now. He told me he used the same principles that alcoholics use to stay sober, and that the Navy Seals use to keep going: "I can't promise that I'll be sober for ever, but I can stay sober today. And that's all I plan to do. Just today." I hope you find that encouraging. I certainly do.

Smartphones and other Screens

Are your phone habits, or those of someone you love, becoming a problem? Unless you set and enforce some boundaries, your smartphone has made you instantly available to anyone who has your email address or phone number. Bosses, colleagues, even friends need to know when it's okay and not okay to call or message (unless it's a genuine emergency). And you need to hold yourself to the same.

Is your smartphone negatively impacting your concentration while studying or your productivity at work? That's a Red Flag. Does your smartphone monopolise your personal time? When you're together, do you look at your phone more than you look at your loved one? Screen addiction is real and it's damaging.

A friend of mine told me how his wife invariably brought her smartphone to bed to check in on social media or to play games before going to sleep. Usually with earphone in her ears. She even slept with it under her pillow. Red Flag. He felt isolated and excluded. She was never too tired to engage with these unknown friends privately online but was often too tired for nookie. He felt as if she was carrying on an affair right there in their bedroom in front of his very eyes. She wasn't, but that was what it felt like to him. And it burned. Smartphones in bed are Red Flags. Believe it.

You already know that a smartphone is probably the primary conduit for online bullying—which can be relentless and public and devastating. Be vigilant about this and put measures in place to protect your family. Also, smartphones can be the primary conduit for porn or flaky world views or extreme politics or crazy conspiracy theories into your home.

You need to think carefully about the role and place of smart phones in your life and in your home. I'll say it again, screen addiction is real and it's damaging. Take the Red Pill. If you or someone you know is addicted, something has to change. Get help.

Money issues

Money is not the most important thing in life. But it's reasonably close. Like oxygen. I mean, you know, when you need it, you *really* do need it. You'd better take it seriously. And you should be very wary of linking yourself to people who don't.

I'm not talking about obsessing over it, or letting it totally rule you, but I am talking about making sure that you are financially literate and disciplined (see chapter 12 for what you need to know). Being reasonably knowledgeable and disciplined about money is a "culture" which you should strive to establish in yourself and in your family.

My grandfather (my dad's dad) never finished high school. Instead, he joined the army and fought in the 1st World War. After his return, he married my grandmother and they lived a simple life with him working on a farm which he did not own. During the Great Depression of the 1930s, he lost his job on the farm and instead supported his family by delivering groceries to people in an old wheelbarrow (something which makes me very proud). He understood the dignity of work and diligence and frugality and perseverance. And they raised five boys, all of whom did finish high school.

My own father joined the air force at the age of 17, straight out of school, to fight in the 2nd World War. After fighting in north Africa and Italy, he came back and went to a technical college. And after forty years of hard work and financial discipline he managed to retire with a house that was paid for and with a pension that supported my mom after he died.

I'm super grateful that I had the opportunity to go to university.

I'm married to a woman with three degrees and we have three children, all of whom have university degrees. We've all had the opportunity to travel internationally, and we're fortunate to live in a comfortable home in a peaceful middle-class neighbourhood. I know full well that all of this is much more about God's grace than about any ability or effort on my part, and I'm very mindful of the fact that these circumstances could change at any moment, but do you see a trajectory here?

The point I'm coming to is this: For most of us, the road to financial security is long and difficult and requires discipline. Sometimes it takes generations of effort and consistently good decision making.

Don't under-estimate this—avoid linking yourself to a life partner or business partner who is financially immature, who has never had good financial roll-models, who's always on the lookout for an easy buck, who can't stick to a budget, who focuses on procuring "stuff" rather than assets.

Gambling is a major Red Flag. I'm not talking about a flutter on the odd big horse race or a few hours of fun at a casino on your annual holiday. But be very aware of joining yourself to people who are proud of their VIP status at a casino, or who gamble online late at night. It's not for nothing that the government views casinos as a convenient way to tax the poor.

Another major Red Flag is when people don't live within their means. They love to shop, they love to eat out, they love to party. They buy fancy clothes and flash cars and go on expensive holidays. And they get into too much debt. Not "good" debt like buying a home or a business. Instead, they max out their credit cards and then get a second card so they can borrow money on that card to pay the minimum instalment on the first card. Avoid people like this at all costs—they are financially illiterate; they have no financial self-discipline and at some point, they will crash and burn financially. Do not get so close that you get caught in the flames.

Now don't get me wrong, you should absolutely spend money reasonably on things and experiences that bring you joy. All I'm saying is be mindful. Think about the long-term impact. And then make a considered decision.

The following example illustrates the point.

PERSON A	PERSON B
Buys Starbucks **COFFEE** every day	Buys Starbucks **STOCK** every day
Spends **$4/day**	Invests **$4/day**
Spends **$80/month**	Invests **$80/month**
Spends **$960/year**	Invests **$960/year**
Spends **$19,200** over **20 years**	Invests **$19,200** over **20 years** with **19% average** annual RIO
RESULT	**RESULT**
Gets a caffeine boost from branded coffee every day	Makes **$161,396** over 20 years
Loses **$19,200**	Makes **$229/month** in dividends

♥ Start **BUYING STOCKS** of the companies you love, not the products

Figure 4: The Starbucks Investor. *Source: Twitter @GrahamStephan*

And finally, never ever ever ever stand surety[3] for someone else's debt.

---

3   To "stand surety" means to assume legal responsibility for someone else's obligations. When you stand surety for someone, you are essentially promising to fulfil their obligations or debts if they are unable to do so themselves.

Career

We work for three reasons: to earn, to learn and to have fun. If any one of these is deficient for too long, then that's a red flag in your career, and for your long-term happiness. Time to move on. If you're not progressing or you're unhappy. Don't whine about it. Act. Move on.

BUT before you do, just remember the 1st Law of Wing Walking: Wing Walking is the daring (insane) act of climbing out of an aeroplane while it's in flight and walking along the wings holding on to whatever you can find. Wing walking originated as an air show stunt in the 1920s. In those days these nutters operated without parachutes and without safety wires. Unsurprisingly, not many of them had to worry about saving for their old age. The 1st Law of Wing Walking is simply this:

———— 66 ————

"Never let go of what you've got until you've got a firm hold of something else".

Figure 5: Billy Bomar and Uva Kimmey of the Howard Flying Circus wing-walking over New York State. 1930. *Credit: Bettmann/Corbis*

The 1st Law of Wing Walking is good advice regarding your job as well. Seriously. Don't underestimate the value of a paycheque when you have a home loan to service and a family to feed. You should *never* leave a job until you've been offered a better one or unless your plans to start your own business are VERY well advanced. We'll talk more about that later.

And another thing, be wary of job hopping—changing jobs too frequently. I'm speaking as someone who has considered many candidates for employment and rejected most of them. High on my checklist is "How often does this person change jobs?". "Too often" suggests that (a) you're unreliable, you don't commit, or (b) you have poor judgment—as evidenced by your inability to secure the right job with the right employer as part of a long-term career development strategy. In short, you're a flight risk and therefore not someone worth investing in.

Rule of thumb: Unless you're in a really toxic environment or your dream job comes along, you should endeavour to stay with an employer for at least three years. Five is preferable. And as you get older, say past your mid-thirties, that duration should probably increase.

In summary ...

I've learned that it's absolutely not bad or negative to be alert for Red Flags in your life, or in the lives of those around you. On the contrary, you should be on the lookout for them. And when you spot them, take responsibility and DO something about them sooner rather than later.

Be especially vigilant of Red Flags in the areas of personal relationships, money and your health. Ignoring flags in these areas can do profound and lasting damage to your quality of life and wellbeing.

#RedFlagsInRelationships
#MoneyRedFlags
#HealthRedFlags

8

YOU'RE NOT AN ONION

When I was in my twenties at university, my friends and I were quite taken with the idea that we needed to "discover who we really, really were". We told ourselves that we wanted to be truly *authentic*, and *real*, and *genuine*, and not *conditioned* (like our parents, poor things) by the world and our upbringing into becoming boring conformists.

To do this, to discover who we really, really were, we had to peel away our narrow, conformist upbringing and cultures, our preconceptions and prejudices and perspectives so that we could discover the true, essential, us that lay below. We had to "peel back the onion" layer by layer in order to allow the hidden core of who we were to emerge. These superfluous layers included the various cultural, demographic, educational, and world-view stereotypes that we had internalized over the years. The idea was that once all the layers were removed, we could finally see our true selves and understand our own essential "pure" beliefs, values, and motivations.

What a load of old rubbish! The truth is that once all the layers are stripped away, just like with an onion, you'll find that there is nothing there! There is no pre-existing essence or core waiting to be discovered. We are not born with an innate set of character traits or predetermined goals and aspirations.

The truth, as I eventually realised, is that instead of peeling away layers, we need to intentionally *build* ourselves into the types of people that we aspire to be. We need to actively decide who we want to be and what we believe in. We need to cultivate our values, goals, and aspirations through intentional searching, reflection and action.

I'm not saying we shouldn't challenge the cultural, demographic, educational, and world-view stereotypes that we have grown up with. On the contrary, these stereotypes can limit our understanding of the world and stunt our own development and happiness. For example, I know a woman—a wonderful wife and mother and leader who had to make the conscious decision NOT to mimic the toxic mothering style of her own mother. This woman knew that there was a better way and, rather than just peeling away an upbringing which she didn't want to propagate, she *built* a new culture in her own home which she had carefully considered, and which reflected who she aspired to be and what she wanted her home to be like.

To challenge negative cultural or family baggage, you need to engage in critical self-reflection and ask yourself what you truly believe and what you aspire to. You need to look beyond the cultural narratives and societal norms that have been "imposed" upon you and ask yourself what you truly value and what you truly want out of life. This process can be difficult and often requires us to confront our own biases and limitations, but it is a necessary step in the journey which ends not with self-discovery, but with self-actualisation.

Therefore, your essential self is not something that pre-exists within you, waiting to be discovered. Instead, it is something that you have to create through ongoing intentional seeking and action—cultivating your own values, character and aspirations.

Your reading of this book is proof that you are already on this journey. Good for you. Keep going. It's a lifelong process, and it's never too late to start.

#CultiveYourTrueSelf #SelfActualisation #WhoYouWantToBe

9

ABOUT FRIENDS

There are surely few things in life as precious as a close friend. Someone who just *gets* you. Someone who you can be honest and open with about (almost) everything. Someone who has seen you at your best and your worst, and who still wants to be a part of your life.

Maybe you're one of the lucky few who made a lasting connection with someone at primary school that will endure through life. But more likely you're like most of us where people come into our lives for a period—their orbits mingle with ours for a while and it's wonderful. And then our orbits slowly drift apart. It's not that we've fallen out of friendship, it's that our lives begin orbiting in different galaxies—one of us moves to a new city or country, one of us becomes immensely wealthy, one of us starts developing life-views that the other just can't relate to. Whatever. And that's okay.

The point I'm coming to is this: even if a close friendship becomes distant over time, it's still worthwhile to make deep, close friends.

Good friends are super important for our wellbeing because they make us better people. They provide emotional support when we need it, they're good for our health, they increase our overall sense of happiness and fulfilment, and they help us to develop a sense of identity and community.

But here's the thing …

Deep friendships take deep effort

It takes time and effort to build a strong, healthy friendship. You know this. Therefore, you need to be intentional about investing into the relationship, and that commitment must be reciprocated or else the thing will stall.

So, you *both* need to make an effort to remain in contact. You *both* need to make time to get together. You *both* need to take an interest in one another's lives. A good friend is someone who you can turn to in times of need, someone who will listen and offer support and advice. A good friend will celebrate your successes and tell you when you're being a klutz. And you must be the same for them.

Your default response when a good friend invites you for coffee should be "yes", and if you must say "no" then immediately schedule a more convenient time. And their default response should be just the same. Friendships are a two-way street with two-way traffic. One way traffic isn't sustainable. You get what I mean. So put in the effort.

Light friendships are important too

"Light" friendships are important too. These are the friendships that may not be as deep as our closest friendships, but they still play an important role in our social lives. They are the people we hang out with casually, the ones we socialise with in a bigger group. These friendships provide a sense of community and connection. They can be tremendous fun and add flavour and diversity to our lives.

Friendships also play an important role in business. Having a network of friends who are also professionals in your field can provide valuable connections and opportunities. These friends can be valuable mentors, offer advice and support, and even open doors to new job or business opportunities. Building strong, professional friendships is an important step in advancing your career or building a business.

All good, and know this …

You will become the average of the 5 people you spend most time with.

You've probably heard this phrase before—it holds a lot of truth. The people we surround ourselves with undoubtedly have a huge impact on our lives. Our friends can shape our thoughts, values, and behaviours—even the way we dress, and the food we eat. Therefore, it's super important to choose our friends wisely. For sure: "bad company corrupts good character"[4].

For example, if you spend a lot of time with people who are financially reckless, you may find yourself becoming more financially reckless as well. If your peer group parties too hard and prioritizes having fun over working, you may find yourself, over time, following suit. And *vice versa* if they're all work and no play. Similarly, if your peer group uses crass language or holds shallow, racist, or sexist views, or disparages education, then you may find yourself adopting these attitudes as well. Or maybe they're just way too negative—they find the problem in every solution; well you may find yourself becoming cynical too.

On the other hand, if your closest friends are people who are emotionally mature, educated, self-aware, self-disciplined, with a high EQ, open to new ideas and different points of view, who value integrity, wisdom, honour, spirituality and kindness, who are fun but not irresponsible; then those characteristics will be reinforced in you too. These types of people will inspire you to become a better, more well-rounded individual—a better version of yourself. And that can have a profound impact on the trajectory of your life, and on that of your children and grandchildren.

Also, the phrase, "*You will become the average of the five people you spend the most time with*" is not limited only to your close friends but also includes people you may interact with on a daily basis, like colleagues, classmates or even family members. Think about that.

---

4   1 Corinthians 15:33

So, when it comes to choosing friends, it's important to consider the values and lifestyles of the people we spend time with. Are they generally positive or generally negative influences? Considering the immense importance of friendships in our lives and the enduring impact that they can have, it's important to take the time to build and nurture relationships wisely. So be discerning and intentional.

——— **66** ———

Here's the secret to dealing with peer pressure—choose the right peers.

—PROF JONATHAN JANSEN

#PositiveInfluence
#ChooseFriendsCarefully
#BeTheFriendYouNeed
#IntentionalFriendships

10

EVERYONE, DO YOUR OWN PUSH-UPS

In the previous chapter we spoke about becoming the average of the five people that we spend most time with, and what a big impact they can have on our lives, both good and bad.

I want to unpack that a bit further: I'm not saying that you should cut everyone out of your life that doesn't have their act together. Afterall, part of our role as humans is to make a constructive contribution to others and to society, to BE a positive influence on those we come into contact with. And also to be open to learning from those that have different views and perspectives and life styles and cultures than our own.

But you should avoid the types of people that routinely bring negativity and drama into your life. These types of people can be toxic and debilitating. They will sap your energy, steal your time, and even drain your resources, and this can hold you back from reaching your own potential or from fulfilling your full responsibilities to your own tribe.

For example, there are people who consistently make bad choices and, inevitably, end up with poor outcomes in their lives. Maybe they are habitual over spenders and are forever in debt. Or maybe they keep getting involved in unhealthy relationships which lead to their tears and pain. Yet, they never learn anything from these experiences. Instead, they do the same thing again and again! And then they expect you to be available to help pick up the pieces. Again.

There's a name for people like that, they're called "askholes"—people who keep asking for advice but never take it. You can't change these people or fix their problems for them. Because they CHOOSE to consistently make bad life choices. I'm sorry if this sounds harsh but don't let them make their problems your problems over and over again.

Better (for both of you) to put some distance between you. They need to grow up and learn to "do their own push-ups". And you need to set some boundaries.

"You can't hire someone else to do your push ups for you."
—JIM ROHN

Then there are the constant complainers, those who always see the negative side of everything and blame others for their problems. They never take responsibility for their own actions (or non-actions)—the classic "victim mentality". Again, you can't change these people or fix their problems.

These types of ongoing negative attitudes are toxic for everyone, them and you. So don't spend too much time in that environment or with those types of people. Instead point them towards professional counselling and then *create distance*.

In short, it's important to have a good balance of positive, supportive and challenging people in your life. These people will help you to grow in mental maturity and life-skills. But you also have to be aware of the types of people who bring unending negativity and drama into your life and keep a healthy and wise distance from them as much as possible.

11

HOW TO MAKE A LIFE PLAN

The concept of a "Life Plan" is not something that I grew up with but I was lucky enough to be introduced to the idea when I was about 30 by my buddy Craig (more on him in Chapter 19).

Having a Life Plan is helpful for a number of reasons:

1. It helps you to identify your goals and aspirations and to create a roadmap to achieve them within a broad timeframe. It gives you a sense of direction and purpose in life.

2. With a clear plan in place, you can focus your energy and efforts on the things that matter. And you can stop wasting your time and energy on stuff that doesn't really matter. In essence, you can stop juggling balls that you shouldn't be juggling and *simplify your life*.

3. A life plan therefore helps you feel more in control of your life, reducing feelings of uncertainty and anxiety.

4. When you have a clear sense of what you want to achieve in life, and by when, it becomes easier to make decisions that align with your goals. And as we know from Chapter 1, the more consistently you make good decisions, the better your outcomes will be.

In short, having a Life Plan is a very good thing, no question.

But we should always make our plans with a healthy dose of humility and reverence for God's greater plans for our lives. Plan by all means, but don't imagine that you can *determine*. We live in a world that is in large measure beyond our control—your Life Plan can be up-ended in an instant if you come off your motorbike, or your child develops leukaemia, or your husband runs away to join the circus. Then you're going to have to gather yourself and slowly develop a new Life Plan. Or maybe, you'll be halfway through your Life Plan and come to realise that it just doesn't suit you anymore, you've changed, and your dreams have changed. Cool. I hope you have the courage to adjust your Life Plan too.

There are lots of different ways to develop a Life Plan and in fact you could have several plans at the same time: one could be focused more on family goals, another on education, a different one on career. For me the handy thing about a Life Plan is that it gives you certain time horizons for action. For instance, in the example below, if Child #1 is born when I'm 29 then, all things being equal, they'll be going to university when I'm 47. Now work backwards: when do I have to start saving (and how much) to afford their fees? And don't forget Child #2 who's a few years behind, and the home loan, and I want to be debt-free by the time I'm 56. Now, what do I need to do for the twenty years *before* that to realise these goals? Hmmm, big questions. Which need some serious thought.

So, use a Life Plan to help you to pace and space important decisions and goals in a way that helps to actually achieve them:

1. A life plan helps you identify your long-term financial goals, such as saving for retirement or buying a home. Once you have a clear idea of your goals and their timeframe, you can create a plan to achieve them and make financial decisions accordingly.

2. With a life plan, you can prioritize your spending based on your goals and values. This will help you avoid overspending on things that don't align with your long-term plans and commitments.

3. A life plan will also help you manage your debt by creating a plan to pay off high-interest debt, such as credit cards or personal loans, and avoid taking on new debt that doesn't align with your goals.

4. A life plan will help you build wealth over time by creating a plan to save and invest your money in a way that aligns with your long-term goals.

Here's an example of a high-level Life Plan: Once you have a broad plan like this in place, you should discuss it with your financial planner who can help you set interim savings and investment goals to help you achieve your life-style goals. Refer to the example on the next page.

My age	Life Dreams	Career development	Our home	Child #1	Child #2	Remarks
25		Engineer in training	Rent a 1-bed apparment			
26						Change jobs for career advancement
27	Get married					Save for 1st home deposit
28		Engineer	Rent a bigger apartment	Birth		
29	Learn to play guitar					
30						
31		Senior Engineer	Buy first home		Birth	Change jobs for career advancement
32	Learn to play golf					
33				Primary School		
34		Get an MBA			Primary School	
35	Learn to ride a horse	Engineering Manager				
36	Learn to fly fish		Buy bigger home			
37	10th Wedding anniversary					
38						
39		Associate Director		High School		
40					High School	
41						
42	Learn to scuba					
43						
44		Director				
45				University		Change jobs for career advancement
46						
47	20th Wedding anniversary				University	Take family on a dream holiday
48						
49						
50	Learn to skydive					Pay off house

Now not everyone resonates with this type of plan. Different styles of Life Plans suit different people, and that's okay. Here's another example:

Life Goals	5 Year Plan	Daily Goals
Career:	**Career:**	**Career:**
-Manage a big company	-Get promoted to manager and look at transfering	-Be the best employee & look for training oppurtnities
-Publish a book	-Complete first draft of my book	-write everyday
Bucket List:	**Bucket List:**	**Bucket List:**
-Become Trilingual	-Be able to hold simple conversations in other lang	-Practice language with flash-cards and games
-See the world	-Go to at least 2 foreign countires	-Save up for passport and travel fare
Financial/Equity:	**Financial/Equity:**	**Financial/Equity:**
-Be debt free	-Owe less than 10k in debt	-pay as much toward debt as I can
-own my own house & car	-buy a house and start payments	-keep an eye out for bargain houses & cars
Family/Social:	**Family/Social:**	**Family/Social:**
-Be happily married	-be married	-go to social events where I can meet or get closer to someone
-raise good kids	-start planning for children	-call my parents for holidays and birthdays
-be on good terms with my parents	-be speaking with parents every month or so	
Personal:	**Personal:**	**Personal:**
-Be physically fit	-get down to 160lbs	-exercise twice a week
-be a patient person	-stop having a hot temper	-count to ten when angry
-be organized and clean	-tidy house	-organize my stuff
-spiritually grounded	-spiritually invested	-spirutally searching

Figure 6. An example of a Goals List
Source: https://purposeadvisory.com.au/blog/f/what-are-the-best-resources-for-creating-a-life-plan

And another ....

Figure 7: An example of a Tree of Life plan *Source: https://purposeadvisory.com.au/blog/f/what-are-the-best-resources-for-creating-a-life-plan*

There are lots of useful Life Planning tools and styles online and I'd really recommend that you check them out and start developing your Life Plan sooner rather than later. Do it together with your spouse. An integrated plan that you both agree on is super cool. And then keep monitoring your progress and adjusting your plan as real life unfolds.

Just for funzies I asked ChatGPT to provide a Life Plan for a 30-year-old male medical doctor, who has recently married, has children at age 32 and 34, wants to become the manager of a medical practice, and retire with a net worth of USD 5 million at age 65. This is what it returned in 3 seconds flat:

Vision: To lead a fulfilling life as a successful medical professional, devoted husband, and loving father, and to retire with a net worth of USD 5 million at age 65.

Short-term Goals (1–3 years), Age 30–33

- Pay off all student loans and other debts.
- Save $20,000 for a down payment on a house.
- Gain experience in a specialized medical field by working as a resident in a hospital.
- Improve communication and leadership skills by taking courses and attending seminars.

Medium-term Goals (4–10 years), Age 33–40.

- Purchase a home in a desirable location.
- Gain more experience and build a reputation as a competent and compassionate medical professional.
- Build a network of professional contacts in the medical field.
- Improve business management and financial skills by taking courses and attending seminars.
- Earn a promotion to a higher position within a medical practice.

Long-term Goals (11–30 years) Age 40–60

- Become a partner in a large medical practice by age 45.
- Start a side business in the medical field, maybe an importer of specialised equipment or diagnostic software.
- Build a diversified investment portfolio with a focus on long-term growth.
- Continue to expand professional network and leadership skills.
- Become the senior partner in a large medical practice by age 55.
- Save aggressively for retirement and aim to retire with a net worth of $5 million at age 60.

> **Monitoring progress:**
> - Track monthly expenses and savings to ensure financial goals are being met.
> - Review progress towards professional goals every year and adjust plans as needed.
> - Revisit the life plan every 3–5 years to assess progress, update goals, and adjust strategies.

Making a life plan is really not difficult. And it's invaluable as a tool to help you to pace and space important milestones in a way that helps to actually achieve your goals and aspirations as opposed to just dreaming about them.

Seriously, do it. ☺

#PlanYourLife
#MakeALifePlan

12

WHAT YOU NEED TO KNOW ABOUT MONEY

When you've grown up in an ordinary middle-class home where your parents worked in someone else's company, as do most of the people you know, then the chances are that you were never exposed to some of the key money lessons that are the difference between becoming financially independent and remaining dependent on either an employer or later, your kids.

Being financially literate does not mean being a financial whizz. It means knowing at least the basics of how to make simple, solid financial decisions.

One reason that people often fail to make good decisions—financial or otherwise—is because those decisions seem too complicated or intimidating. Simplicity in life is a thing to strive for.

Will the simple solution always lead to the best outcomes? No. But generally it does produce a better outcome than either just avoiding the problem or doing something stupid.

If you're anything like me, you know how important it is to make good financial decisions. You've even visited a financial advisor. The problem is they all speak a strange foreign language that no one can understand—"buy this smoothed flexi endowment or that deferred tax portfolio annuity." What?! It's all just too exhausting. And so, like a deer in the headlamps, you either do nothing or you just blindly follow whatever advice the salesman gives you.

Wouldn't it be great if there were a few simple, universal rules that everyone could understand and which you could scribble on a post-it and stick on the fridge? Financial wisdom that, if followed consistently, would assure your long-term financial prospects.

Luckily, such a set of rules does actually exist. Harold Pollack, a University of Chicago public policy professor, was conducting an online interview with Helaine Olen, author of Pound Foolish, a book about the financial advice industry. To show that financial advice is overly complex, Pollack took an index card and jotted down nine basic financial rules that cover almost everything that the average person needs to know. The image was shared worldwide, picked up by countless media outlets, and now it's been expanded into an "index card" book that Pollack co-authored with Olen.

READ THIS ...

This chapter is based on the book: *The Index Card: Why Personal Finance Doesn't Have to Be Complicated* by Harold Pollack and Helaine Olen. It's a truly freeing read for anyone who feels lost about their finances. Inside is an easy-to-follow action plan that works in good times and bad, giving you the tools, knowledge, and confidence to seize control of your financial life.

LISTEN TO THIS ...

If you prefer an audio summary on your daily commute, then listen to: *https://freakonomics.com/podcast/everything-always-wanted-know-money-afraid-ask* Freakonomics Radio Podcast (episode 298). Everything you always wanted to know about money (but where too afraid to ask).

The rules covered in the book are simple, even obvious—and that's the beauty. There's no magic fix or hot-shot investment. Instead, the authors point you toward basic investment concepts like save (for a long time), pay-off your debts, and buy a house as your primary retirement investment.

The rules are:

All the financial advice you'll ever need on one card
Rule #1 Strive to save 10 to 20 percent of your income
Rule #2 Pay your credit card balance in full every month
Rule #3 Max out your 401(k) and other tax-advantaged savings accounts
Rule #4 Never buy or sell individual stocks
Rule #5 Buy indexed mutual funds and exchange-traded funds
Rule #6 Make your financial advisor commit to the fiduciary standard
Rule #7 Buy a home when you are financially ready
Rule #8 Insurance: Make sure you're protected
Rule #9 Do what you can to support the social safety net
Rule #10 Remember the index card

Let's unpack them ...

Rule No. 1: Save 10 to 20% of your income

Do this with your very first pay-cheque. And if you missed doing it with your first cheque, then start it now. Immediately. And I don't mean "save for a nice holiday/car/TV/outfit etc" and then spend it". I mean save 10–20% of every bit of income you ever get from now on. And don't touch it! Until you retire.

But don't just park it in a bank savings account; the interest that your bank pays you is ALWAYS lower than the inflation rate, so your money loses value over time. Instead, invest in your company's retirement plan and/or save into a private Retirement Fund (also called a *Retirement Annuity* (RA) or an *Individual Retirement Account* (IRA)). More on this in Rule No.3.

Rule No. 2: Pay-off your credit card in full every month

This may be the most important single rule on the card for a lot of people. If you're carrying a credit card balance, PAY IT OFF as if your financial future depended on it! The reason is simple: the credit card company charges you a LOT of interest for the privilege of using their money (20% and more).

Think of it like this: you're paying them 20% of the outstanding balance on your card using your after-tax earnings! Whereas, if you pay the balance in full every month then you're paying zero interest. And if you're saving your 10–20% of income then you're earning interest on that saving (say 5%). That's a swing of 25% to the upside! You're very unlikely to ever make that return consistently on any investment in your life!

Credit cards and other high-interest loans are the single biggest reason that so many people remain trapped in financial distress. Pay your cards off as soon as possible! Do everything you possibly can to pay them off and then, if you have difficulty sticking with this rule, cut up the card!

Finally, avoid all those store cards and loyalty cards that offer extended payment terms on purchases, they're just credit cards by another name. They're ALL designed to tempt you to buy more and pay interest to the issuer.

Rule No. 3: Maximise your contributions to the retirement plan run by your employer. As well as any other tax-advantaged savings accounts

Today most retirement plans are called *Provident Funds* (401(k) funds in the USA). If you are formally employed your employer will generally require that you join the company Provident Fund. All the employees in the company will contribute to the fund and the total contributions will be invested in stocks (shares), bonds, and cash by a specialist investment firm. Your share of this total contribution along with any growth will however always be identifiable and will remain only yours and be available to you when you retire.

The advantage of a Company Provident fund is that, since the total contributions of all the employees, can be quite a large amount, the investment fees charged by the specialist investment firm will be lower than if you were to invest with the same firm on your own. Also, very often your employer will kick in a matching contribution, so the more you contribute, the more your employer contributes.

Most companies will limit the proportion of your income that you may contribute to their Provident Fund—find out what the top limit is and choose it unless it is truly unaffordable! Remember your goal is to save 10 to 20 percent of your total income every month (Rule No. 1).

For those who are self-employed or whose employer does not offer a company retirement plan, Provident Funds (sometimes called Retirement Annuities (RA's) or Individual Retirement Accounts (IRA's)) are also available directly from a Financial Investment Firm. Typically, you just set up a payment order on your bank account and invest the same amount every month automatically. As with company retirement funds, the money that you invest in a Retirement Annuity is tax deductible (up to certain limits). This means that whatever you invest in your retirement fund is deducted from your taxable income before you pay tax—so in addition to saving, you also pay less tax.[5]

There are also other tax-advantaged savings options: Many countries allow you to deposit money (up to certain limits every year) into *Tax Free Savings Accounts*. These are offered by many banks and financial institutions. You must definitely check them out—just google "tax free savings" in your country.

And by the way, unless it's genuinely a case of survival, never ever

---

5   In most countries you will pay some tax on your retirement savings once you
     start using them. So tax is effectively deferred until after your retirement.

EVER take money out of your retirement fund prior to retirement. If you do that you will destroy the compounding effect of your investment and it will be almost impossible to catch up again (see Rule No.5 for a full explanation of the "compounding effect"). And to make matters even worse, your retirement fund is likely to levy "early withdrawal" penalties which will further reduce the value of your investment.

Rule No. 4: Never buy or sell individual stocks

For most of us ordinary Joes, there are better and less risky ways to invest than by buying and selling individual stocks (so called "active trading"). For the simplest, re-read Rule No. 3! However, if you've already maxed out the contribution that you are allowed to make to your company retirement fund, *and* you're debt free *and* you've still got some spare cash to invest, then read on.

First, a dose of reality: It's naive to imagine that you can outperform specialist investment firms over the long term. Do you really think that you can beat teams of highly specialised brainiacs who have 24/7 access to the best market intel, investment strategies, risk management and research tools, by spending a few hours after work trawling Google and YouTube? If your answer to that question is "yes", you're dreaming. Sorry. Swallow the red pill.

Bottom line: in the long run, most individuals who pick stocks for a living underperform even the average return of the market. And they pay serious transaction costs for the privilege of doing that.

And it gets worse: even employing "expert" financial gurus to actively trade stocks on your behalf may not result in above-average returns. And the reason is simple, who do you think is paying for their fancy offices and lifestyles and annual bonuses? You!

In fact, countless studies have shown that even the majority of professional "active" fund managers fail to beat the wider market average consistently over the long run. And yet they charge you for their expertise!

In all likelihood, it's a much better idea to …

Rule No. 5: Buy inexpensive, well-diversified index funds and exchange-traded funds

There is plenty of research which indicates that in the long-term it is better for the average Joe, who is debt free, to invest in a *low-cost, diversified index fund. And then to HOLD it for the long-term.*

So, what is an index fund?

Index funds, also known as Tracker funds, Exchange Traded Funds or as "passive" funds—don't try to beat the market. Instead, they automatically track the performance of different market Indices. The tracker fund buys shares in the companies which make up the index, generally in the same proportion as their weighting in the index.

So, a "Top 100" tracker fund copies the composition and performance of the Top 100 Company Stocks on a given stock exchange (the Top 100 Index), with the goal of delivering the same annual return as the index (before costs are deducted).

There are lots of different types of Indices on most stock markets: The S&P 500 index tracks the performance of the top 500 shares on the New York Stock exchange. Similarly, you can choose more sector-focused indices like, property, or technology, or commodities, or construction or energy.

What are the pros and cons of index funds?

The big advantage of passive investing is cost: a tracker fund can have an annual charge of 0. 1% to 0.4%. An actively managed fund could easily charge five or ten times as much, with no guarantee it will beat the index (as we've discussed, most don't over time).

> **LISTEN TO THIS …**
>
> To find out more about how significant the differences between passive (low-cost index) and actively managed investing can be over time, listen to the Freakonomics Radio Podcast (episode 297) *The Stupidest Thing You Can Do With Your Money*: https://freakonomics.com/podcast/stupidest-money

Critics of index funds often point out that index funds simply follow the market up or down, whereas "active" managers can rotate out of risky stocks in a downturn and so mitigate losses and also pile into running stocks in an upturn and so accelerate gains. That is their sales pitch and it's true. But, given that actively-managed funds struggle to beat the market over the long-term *and* are more expensive, it's easy to see why tracker funds and passive investing have taken off in a big way in the last decade or so.

Returning to the point that, for the average Joe, it is better to invest in a *low-cost, diversified index fund. And then to HOLD it for the long-term:*

The logic is this: Holding an index investment for the "long-term" means that you capitalize on the magic of compounding returns without succumbing to the tyranny of the high costs associated with actively managed investments.

So, what are "compounding returns"?

Albert Einstein once said that Compound Interest is the most powerful force in the universe. Take a look at Example 1 in the illustration on page 74 let's say you invest $100 in Year 1 and nothing more after that. And let's say you earn 10% interest on that sum in the first year, then by the end of that year you will have $100 x 1.1 = $110. You made $10, congratulations. Now you STAY INVESTED, so at the end of the second year you have $110 x 1.1 = $121. You made $11 in year two, i.e. *more* than you made in the previous year. And so on. Every year you make more than you made in the previous year. The longer you remain invested the more your growth will "compound" and accelerate.

In a little over seven years, your $100 will be worth $200! In year 20 you'll make $61 compared to the $1 you made in year 1, and by the end of year 20 your $100 initial investment will have grown to $673. That's 6.73 times the money you put in!

Compound interest can be given a shot of steroids if instead of investing just a single once-off amount, you invest $100 a year, every year, repeatedly.

Take a look at Example 2 in the illustration on page 74: at the same interest rate of 10% as above, after 7 years you will have $1 044 to your name, nearly 1.5x the amount you put in. And the longer you just keep doing the same thing, the more your investment will "compound" itself—after 20 years you'll have invested $2000 but you will be worth over $6 300—3.15 times the total amount that you put in.

Now compare that with investing $200 every year for only ten years, see Example 3. In total you will have invested $200 x 10 = $2000 (same as Example 2 above). Then at the same interest rate of 10% as above, after 10 years your investment will be worth $3 506, only 1.75x your total input and only 55% of the value in Example 2.

That is the power of compound interest. And why you should start your retirement savings as soon as possible and then HOLD for the long term.

As **Warren Buffet**, perhaps the world's most successful investor, is fond of advising: "Don't try to "time" the market. The best time to invest was 10 years ago, the second-best time is today. Time IN the market beats TIMING the market. Every time. My advice: buy the index and then HOLD it."

THE POWER OF COMPOUNDING

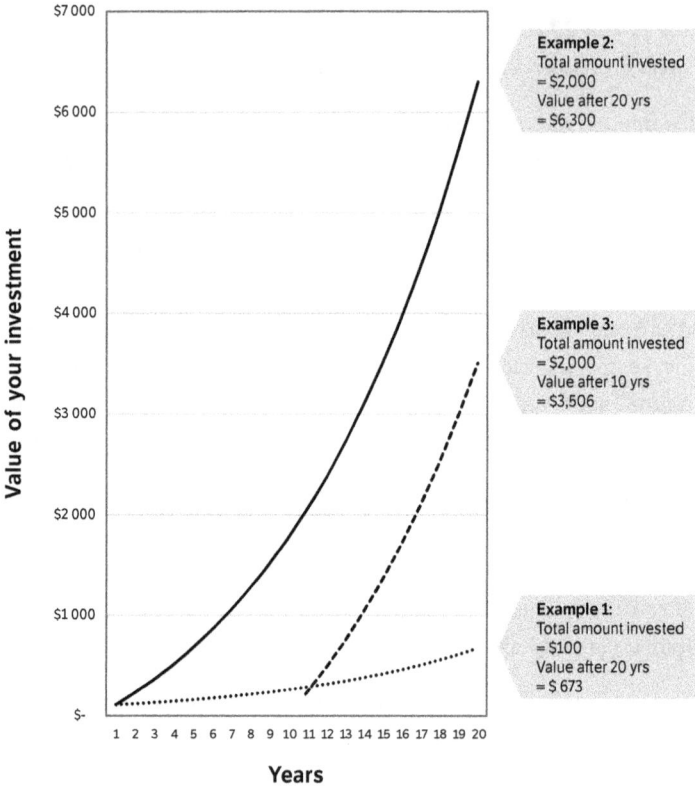

Example 2:
Total amount invested
= $2,000
Value after 20 yrs
= $6,300

Example 3:
Total amount invested
= $2,000
Value after 10 yrs
= $3,506

Example 1:
Total amount invested
= $100
Value after 20 yrs
= $ 673

Value of your investment

Years

...... **Example 1:** You invest $100 in year 1 and nothing more.

——— **Example 2:** You invest $100 every year.

- - - **Example 3:** You invest $200 every year for ten years. But you start late.

Rule No. 6: Make your financial advisor commit to the fiduciary standard

Obviously, it can be really hard for the average person to take in and execute all this investment advice on their own. So you might consider hiring a financial advisor. But not just any financial advisor—just because they work for a financial company—remember, their goal is to make money for themselves, usually by charging you fees.

Make sure your financial advisor belongs to a regulatory body to which he is ethically and professionally accountable and which has certified his competence.

In the United States, the fiduciary standard is a federal requirement designed to ensure that financial advisors don't sell clients products that are better for the advisors than for the clients. Other countries have their own such bodies—make sure your financial advisor is signed-up!

This is not meant to besmirch the reputation of all financial advisors. It's also worth noting that sometimes, it may be the advisors who try to keep their clients on the right track. Experience shows that, left to their own devices, after three years people get bored. So they start looking for a little fun, a little action, and "Hey, maybe we should sell down on this long-term conservative portfolio and start dabbling in more exciting individual stocks, or buy a flashier car etc etc." A good financial advisor will discourage that behaviour and keep you focussed on the long-term goal of financial independence.

Okay then, moving on to the single-biggest expenditure that most of us will ever think about …

Rule No. 7: Buy a home when you are financially ready

Most of us have been conditioned from birth to believe that you're not a full adult until you own a home. But you need to be careful about that. True, you do need a roof over your head. And also true that there is something deep inside most of our psyche which says, especially if you have a family, that you should be the owner of your roof—it definitely gives a sense of security and roots and emotional solidity.

However, it's also true that your home is likely to be the single asset for which you will take on the most debt in your life. It will also be the most undiversified investment you're ever going make. It will also have the highest transaction costs (bond costs, transfer fees, agents commission etc).

So, you don't want to rush into buying a home and you want to buy a home in a very sensible way.

"Sensible" means:

1. **Save before buying** so that you can put down at least 10% of the purchase price as a deposit. The more you can put down, the better terms you are likely to be able to negotiate with your lending institution and the faster you can pay-off the loan.

2. **Budget fully and realistically.** One of the trickiest things about buying a home is figuring out exactly how much it will cost you. Apart from the monthly mortgage re-payment, you will be paying for property taxes and insurance and maintenance and utilities and furnishings. And you will need an emergency fund for when the roof leaks or the plumbing gets clogged etc etc etc.

3. As a general rule of thumb, you should **restrict your home mortgage repayment to no more than 25% to 30% of your gross monthly income**, or no more than 2.5 to 3 times your annual salary. This includes not only the mortgage payment but also additional costs such as property taxes, insurance, and maintenance fees.

4. It's natural to want to buy the nicest home possible and therefore to maximise your re-payments. Many couples buy a house based on applying the above rule of thumb to both their incomes. That's okay if you're both happy to be committed to the work

treadmill for many years. And you've considered what you'll do when you fall pregnant etc.

5. Finally of course, this rule of thumb is just a guideline and will vary based on the interest rate on your home loan (what if it goes up?) and your personal circumstances (do you have extraordinary costs—medical bills, child-care bills etc that Joe Soap doesn't have?). It's crucial to do a comprehensive analysis of your finances and budget (see Rule #10) before making a final decision on the maximum mortgage repayment you can afford.[6]

6. **Maintenance is NOT an optional item**. The amount of maintenance your home needs can hinge on factors like age, size, and construction (is it a thatch roof, are the walls made of wood or brick etc). The general convention is that home maintenance will cost 1% to 4% of your property's value each year. So apply your mind and don't allow your biggest investment to degrade by skimping on maintenance—that is false economy.

7. **Pay down your home loan as fast as you possibly can.** Every spare cent you have should go into your home loan. Re-read Rule No. 2. And the section above on Compound Interest. The same principles apply to home loans. Depending on the prevailing interest rates, if you pay just 5% more than the minimum monthly repayment into your home loan, you can shorten a 20-year repayment period by roughly 3 years AND save roughly 10% of the total value of the loan in interest payments.

---

6   Some Red Pill news here: If you fail to honour your home loan repayments, the bank is entitled to re-possess your home. They'll then sell it at a knock-down price and, once they've covered every cost they can think of, they'll give you what is left over—normally a pittance of the value of the property. And your credit history will be very badly scarred. Do NOT just stop paying the mortgage payment, rather go and meet with the bank, explain the situation to them, try to negotiate a payment holiday or an extended re-payment term or sell the place yourself. Any of these will have a far better outcome than just defaulting on the repayments.

8. In many ways, one of the best things about buying a home is that the mortgage re-payment is a kind of forced savings plan. This is only true if you **DO NOT dip into your home equity** for anything other than a real emergency. Accessing "excess" value in your home loan account defeats the objectives of point 5 above. Now of course lending institutions know this and love it. They will go to great lengths to lend you as much money as possible so that you can pay them as much interest as possible for as long as possible. Resist. DO NOT dip into your home equity for anything other than a real emergency.

That's, "buy a home when you're financially ready."

Rule No. 8: Insurance. Make sure you're protected

The purpose of insurance is to make sure that you are protected if you have a *life-changing* event, not an *inconvenient* event:

You don't need **homeowners' insurance** for the inconvenience when your seven-year-old hits a ball through the kitchen window. You do need homeowners' insurance for when the tree falls and your whole kitchen gets taken out[7].

You don't need **medical insurance** for a visit to your doctor. You do need medical insurance in case you land-up in hospital for an extended period or in ICU for even a relatively short period. Or perhaps if you have a chronic condition that requires expensive, ongoing medication.

You do need **liability insurance** if you own a car, in case you take out some guy's Mercedes Benz or (heaven forbid) you seriously injure someone. When buying motor vehicle insurance always compare the

---

7   Good news: if you have a mortgage (bond) on your home, it will probably include some level of home insurance on the building itself against things like a landslide or subsidence or fire. Check it out with your mortgage provider.

costs of "comprehensive" cover and "third-party, fire and theft" cover. The latter is the minimum you should have.

You do need **life and disability insurance** to protect you and your family in case you get severely injured and become unable to work, or in case your dependents need support after you die[8].

So, remembering that insurance is required to guard against the big things, not the little things:

Decide on what insurance you REALLY need.

1. Shop around and get several comparative quotes. And resist the strong "up-selling" pressure that you are likely to be subjected to.
2. Re-assess your insurance needs annually. Remember that the value of your car depreciates every year. Therefore, so should the cost of your car insurance.
3. Opt for the largest deductible[9] that you can. Your insurance premium will be MUCH lower if your pay for all the little things yourself and only look to your insurer for the life-changing event.
4. Put the savings you achieve by applying the above into your home loan or retirement fund.

---

8 Good news: often your company pension/provident fund (see Rule # 3) will include life and disability insurance at very cost-effective rates. You'll need more (say 5 times your annual salary) if you have a young family for whom losing your income would be a disaster; less if you're married to a financially independent spouse and the children have left home.

9 A deductible is the amount of money that you are responsible for paying toward an insured loss. When a disaster strikes your home or you have a car accident, the deductible is subtracted, or "deducted," from what your insurance pays toward the claim. The larger the deductible, the less you pay in premiums for an insurance policy.

Rule No. 9: Support the social safety net

Pollack says a lot of people don't like Rule No. 9. But he thought it was essential to include, for several reasons. And I agree.

It's important to pay your taxes. For the good of everyone. Indeed, for many people, state-sponsored hospitals and doctors are their only option for essential medical care and social grants are their ticket to a meal. Over and above taxes, it's important to support churches or charities or NGO's that help to make communities into kinder, more caring, more humane places. Whether you are religious or not, I believe this to be a moral imperative.

Super cool. And thanks to Mr Pollack for all that wisdom.

Now I'd like to be so bold as to suggest a final Rule ….

Rule No. 10: Draw up a Budget. And stick to it

So now that you know what to spend your money on, it's important for you to develop a framework to help you stay disciplined and on track—it's called a budget.

Budgets help us to *pre-plan* exactly what we're going to allow ourselves to spend on all the different necessities and nice-to-haves of life. The point is to make sure that (a) we are not spending more than we earn (to avoid going into debt), and (b) that we spend our income in a responsible way that includes retirement saving etc.

There are lots of examples of typical household budgets online and I've also included one on page 82. Microsoft Excel even has some free budget templates that you can download: ***https://create.microsoft.com/en-us/templates/budgets.***

Start by filling in your Gross Income (total earnings). Then take away taxes and any deductions that your company makes (like pension fund contributions etc) to end up with your Net Income (i.e. your "take-home" amount). Now list all your monthly expenses—everywhere your money goes in a typical month. And add these all up to get your Total Expenses.

Naturally your Net Income must be more than your Total Expenses or else you're slowing descending into debt.

Now don't be discouraged, it's almost certain you will really struggle to get this right on your first go. You'll be amazed and probably dismayed at how expensive living can be! But keep at it, cut some expenses and try again. Maybe try the popular **50/30/20 recipe of budgeting** which advises you to save 20% of your income every month. That leaves 50% for needs, including essentials like mortgage or rent and food. The remaining 30% of your income is for discretionary spending. Do whatever you need to do to ensure that your Total Expenses remain less than your Net Income.

Eventually you'll get there, even if it means that you prove to yourself that you can't afford that house or car or vacation *at this time*. Even that is progress toward growing your financial maturity and discipline.

Balancing a budget and sticking to it is a big step towards financial maturity. You won't regret it. Well done.

And remember Rule No. 2: Pay-off your credit card balance in full every month.

See the following page for an example budget with references back to Pollack's Rules.

TYPICAL HOUSEHOLD BUDGET

INCOME	AMOUNT	REMARKS
Gross Monthly Income		
Deductions		
Tax		Get professional help to legally minimise Tax
Company Retirement Fund		**See Rule No. 1 & 3** Aim to save 10–20% of your income.
Medical Insurance (Medical Aid)		**See Rule No. 8** Consider your family situation.
NET Income (Take-home pay)		

EXPENDITURE	AMOUNT	REMARKS
Charitible Giving		**See Rule No. 9** Target 10% of your Net Monthly Income
Recipients XYZ		
Long-Term Investments		**See Rule No. 1 & 3** Top-up your contribution to your Company retirement fund so that your Total Retirement Investments equates to 10–20% of your Income
Other Investment 1		
Other Investment 2		
Home Loan & Maint.		**See Rule No. 7** Restrict your home loan repayment to no more than 25% to 30% of your gross monthly income. This includes property taxes (rates), insurance and maintenance costs. Allow for maintenance costs of 1% to 4% of your property's value each year.
Home Loan Repayments (Or Rent)		
Maintenance		
Household Expenses		**Note 1:** You'll see that there is no line item for credit cards. If you use your credit card for any of these expenses. You must pay it off IN FULL every month.
Groceries, cleaning products etc		
Maid & Gardener		
Water, Energy, Taxes and Refuse		
Phones & Internet		
Furnishings & Décor		**Note 1:** See above
Education Fees		

EXPENDITURE	AMOUNT	REMARKS
Short Term Insurance		
Short Term Insurance (Cars, home etc)		**See Rule No. 8**
Life Insurance		
Medical		If not already deducted from your Gross Income by your company.
Medical Insurance		
Other medical costs		**Note 1:** See above
Vehicles & Fuel		
Car Repayments		
Fuel & Tolls (Train /bus)		**Note 1:** See above
Maintenance		**Note 1:** See above
Other		
Short Term Savings (Vacations etc)		
Entertainment (TV, Resaurants etc)		**Note 1:** See above
Bank Charges		Automatic deduction from your bank account by your bank.
Other		**Note 1:** See above
TOTAL EXPENSES	-	
MONTHLY CASH BALANCE	-	Net Income minus Total expenses must be positive

13

GLOW UP

B rand matters! We all know this. It's the reason Gucci bags, Rolex watches, and Mercedes Benzes can sell for so much more than the equivalent products of some of their competitors. They're not necessarily that much better as actual products but their *brands* have incredible pull.

Companies know that good branding promotes success. It sets them apart from the competition. It tells people about their core values—things like quality, safety, reliability, professionalism, adventure. A strong brand helps customers know what to expect. And good branding leads to greater demand and higher sales margins.

It's just the same with you. A good personal brand (aka *reputation*) will help you advance in every situation. A bad personal brand will drag you down, hinder your career and hamper your pulling power with babes or eligible bachelors.

I can't emphasise this enough. You need to think carefully about the impressions that your looks, language, values and behaviour leave on those around you.

You need to be intentional and make an effort. You (we all) need to *glow up*.

Dress for Success

Be under no illusions, looks do count. First impressions are important. Classy is cool. So, dress well and appropriately for every occasion. Sloppy clothes suggest a sloppy attitude. I'm not talking expensive, I'm talking neat, clean, ironed. Not too sexy. Not too showy. Not like a slob. Make an effort.

Consider your posture. Consider your weight. Consider your hairstyle. And whether you should have a beard. Or wear make-up (and how much). Consider what getting a face tattoo or a piercing says about your brand. Or wearing your cap backwards, or sideways, or your trousers halfway down your backside.

I'm not saying what may be right or wrong for your sub-culture or your future aspirations, I'm just saying that looks are important in branding. And you need to be intentional.

Language

Think about the way you talk—what you say and how you say it. What comes out of a person's mouth and the tonality of their speech is a direct reflection of their character.

There's an old idiom that says, "sticks and stones can break my bones, but words cannot hurt me". It's total garbage. Words are incredibly important. Affirming and encouraging words propel people to do better, be better, live better. Harsh and unkind or unfair words can crush your spirit and lead to bitterness and resentment. Build your brand as someone whose words build others up rather than break them down.

Bad language is a bad idea. Always. It suggests that you lack self-control, are aggressive, inconsiderate and impolite. Definitely not classy. For the same reasons, shouting and screaming in anger is a bad idea. Always.

Think also about the pitch of your voice (lower is generally better), the speed with which you speak (slower is generally better), and the volume with which you speak (loud and brash suggests arrogance and self-centeredness, it's a real turn-off in most cultures).

Manners

Good manners are about respecting yourself and others. People, those that count, prefer people with good manners. People with good manners make a positive impression on those around them. In other words, good manners are an important part of building a positive personal brand.

What constitutes good manners may differ between cultures, but the list below is common to most. You should practice them all. Especially if you have children. Reality check: *Children will emulate what you say and do. do. Not what you tell them to do.*

So,

1. Be polite. Say 'Please' when you ask for something and 'Thank You' when you receive something.
2. Ask before taking anything that is not yours. And be sure to return it in good condition with proper thanks when you're done.
3. Apologise when you've done something wrong or hurt someone's feelings (even if it was inadvertent). And be genuine about it. Empathy is a life-skill that is incredibly attractive.
4. Cover your mouth when you cough or sneeze. Chew with your mouth closed—no one wants to see your lunch once it's left your fork. And never pick your nose in public.
5. Know when and how to enter a conversation without interrupting anyone.
6. Don't point your finger at someone when speaking to them—it's very confrontational, aggressive even.
7. Clean up after yourself. Be helpful around the house and at the office. In fact, wherever you are.

8. Never allow your mental faculties to be impaired by drugs or alcohol. Personally, I enjoy a drink or two with friends as much as anyone. But I decided long ago to never get drunk. I just don't trust myself not to do something rude or embarrassing or stupid or hurtful to others. And I'd really regret that. My family don't deserve it.

All of these can be summed up in the timeless ...

Golden Rule: Do unto others as you'd like them to do unto you.

Values

Your values are an incredibly important part of your personal brand and reputation. People will sense them by watching what you say, how you say it, how you treat others and how you conduct your personal and professional affairs. Your *values* are perhaps the most important part of your personal brand. Here are the top five:

- **Trustworthiness:** Being honest, reliable, and consistent in your actions and words builds trust with others, which is essential to a good reputation. Gaining a reputation as someone who can't be fully trusted is the kiss of death to your personal brand. And to career advancement. And to a happy marriage.
- **Respectfulness:** Treating others with respect, regardless of their status or position, demonstrates that you are a person of integrity and good character. Show respect for older people, remember you'll get there too one day. Be kind to people with disabilities. Don't patronise or condescend. Treat everyone with dignity.
- **Responsibility:** Taking ownership of your actions and being accountable for your mistakes shows that you are a responsible and mature individual.
- **Empathy:** Being able to understand and relate to the feelings and perspectives of others is a key component of building strong relationships and a positive reputation. Never make fun of anyone else.

Far better to laugh with someone than at someone. Never be a bully or ignore bullying. Honour lies in protecting the weak, not exploiting them.

- **Competence:** Demonstrating a high level of skill or knowledge in your field of expertise or chosen activities says a lot about you: you're able to commit, you can persevere, you've got a brain, you can turn theory into practice. We'll talk more about competence later.

As a leader, in your home, in the netball team, at work, you should understand that you cast a "leadership shadow": you set a tone by how you behave and how you speak and what you say and how you treat others. And everyone "under" you will see that and emulate you. If you disrespect your wife, don't expect your children to respect her (or later, theirs). If you arrive late for work every morning, don't expect your subordinates to be any different, etc etc. You get the picture.

Great leaders consistently MODEL the culture they want to embed. They do this because they know that behaviour gets caught, not taught.

#GlowUp
#BuildAPersonalBrand
#Manners
#GoldenRule
#Values
#Trustworthy
#Respect
#Responsible
#OwnIt
#Empathy

14

BUILD RAPPORT

rapport

/raˈpɔː/

noun

a close and harmonious relationship in which the people or groups concerned understand each other's feelings or ideas and communicate well.

A large part of building a positive personal brand is developing good relationships with people that you come into contact with. And a large part of that will depend on your skills of interaction, how you communicate, your conversation.

In conversation be interested, and interesting

The art of conversation encompasses many aspects but perhaps it can all be summed up in just two objectives:

1. Be interested

If you haven't already noticed it, you soon will: people are mostly interested in themselves. They love nothing more than to talk about their own interests and dreams and aspirations and fears and careers and irritations and love lives and achievements and children and spouses. So start with them. Listen to them. Be genuinely interested in their world and pretty soon you will find that people just love talking to you. Naturally, there are a few caveats here, beware the social leeches—people who are perpetual whiners, or gossips, or complete bores. These guys will wear you out and bring you down. Or worse, start to rub-off on you.

Also, be discrete. There is nothing worse than confiding in someone and then finding that what was told in confidence is now in the public domain. Warning lights always go off on my mental dashboard when someone tells me something gossipy about someone else—I know they will probably do the same about me at some point.

2. Be interesting

You need a few stock topics that you know a bit about and which people will be interested in—for example, keep abreast of the news, or sports (see next section), or music, or dogs, or business. If you can hit on a common interest with someone, you're well on your way to lasting rapport. Avoid talking about other people unless it's to relate something positive about them.

READ THIS …

How to win friends and influence people by Dale Carnegie. One of the best-selling books of all time, the rock-solid, time-tested advice in this book has carried thousands of people up the ladder of success in their business and personal lives. Do yourself a favour and read it.

How to Talk to Anyone: 92 Little Communication Tricks for Big Success in Relationships by Leil Lowndes. This is a great book to help you master the art of verbal communication in your personal life and in business. An easy read.

At work

Building rapport with colleagues, bosses, subordinates, customers and counterparts is incredibly important to growing your career. The communication skills which we touched on above (*be interested, and interesting*) are just as valid in the workplace, but there are a few additional things to consider:

Primary amongst these is EQ. We've discussed this before, but I cannot emphasise it enough. In the long run, your EQ *WILL* determine the trajectory of your career. So, study the topic like your comfortable retirement depends on it. Strive to be the person that everyone else wants on their team. Because you work hard, you're reliable, you're competent, you're pleasant, you're easy to get along with and you encourage improvement.

But, have a spine! Learn to say no (politely) when you should. Learn to give your honest view (politely) even when it may run contrary to everyone else's.

The other area of communication which is incredibly important at work is your ability to influence others positively. Your ability to influence or persuade people positively to a particular course of action is a massively important part of your career growth. There are lots of skills to be learned here, including the art of being an excellent listener. But it all starts with rapport.

Check out the reading panel below for two brilliant books on this topic. They are must-reads for anyone interested in understanding human behaviour and improving their ability to influence others through the skill and art of communication.

READ THIS ...

Influence: The Psychology of Persuasion by Robert B. Cialdini. This highly acclaimed bestseller explains the psychology of why people say yes and how to apply these principles ethically in business and everyday situations. You'll learn the six universal principles of influence and how to use them to become a skilled persuader—and, just as importantly, how to defend yourself against dishonest influence attempts.

The new Articulate Executive: Look, Act and Sound Like a Leader, by Granville N. Toogood. The simple truth is this: You need to look, act, and sound like a leader to succeed in today's business world. Whether you are giving a speech, making a presentation, conducting a meeting, or simply talking one-on-one, these tried-and-true communication techniques are guaranteed to help you step up your game and speak like a pro.

#BuildRapport
#ArtofPersuasion
#ArtOfConversation

15

WHY SPORT

To love sport is to love life—youth and beauty and skill and joy and resilience. It's a great way to make friends and it can teach us lots of important life lessons, like how to deal with triumph and disappointment (and to not be too phased by either), and self-discipline and dedication. It builds character and self-control. It teaches us about the importance of being a team player (surely one of the most important life lessons). And it's fun!

Sport for Rapport

Even if you don't actively play sport, you should be interested and informed enough to have a light conversation on, say, three different sports. Sport is a great conversation lubricant in the office or when meeting new people or around the fire with your friends. And as we've seen above, building rapport is an incredibly important part of making both personal and professional friends and acquaintances.

It doesn't really matter which three sports you choose, so long as they're commonly supported in your circle. In your chosen three, you should know something about the top three players or teams and the most important tournaments for each sport.

As an example, let's take …

Golf

I know very little about golf. To be frank, I'm a total hack. For starters, the rules are way too complicated. Football is the world's most popular sport because even my granny can understand the offside rule. And, more importantly, everyone can understand the simple logic that when a team scores, they get a point. And at the end, the team with the most points wins.

Not so with golf. In golf, the *lowest* score wins. And the winner buys the drinks. Huh? And then they throw in things called birdies, and eagles and bogies (thankfully the last one is not what you might at first think).

To make matters worse, besides all the different scoring systems that you can choose from—stroke play, match play, scramble, shamble, stableford etc etc, you have the added joy of discovering that they change the rules on different courses ("course rules") and even from day-to-day on the same course! Better still, you can get a *handicap* which, if it's bad enough, can help you to beat a better player (who has a lesser handicap). What? It's all very confusing. Which is largely what makes golf endlessly good as a topic for conversation.

Golf courses themselves are a gift from God. To be able to wander about in an uncrowded, park-like environment for four or five hours in the middle of a city is a joy not to be ignored. It's also an incredibly social game which, like most competitive sports, brings out the best and the worst in its participants. Therefore, it's a good exposer of character. Yours, and those you play with.

Golf is generally quite an expensive sport and so is associated with the more affluent elements of society—businesspeople, aspiring businesspeople, and retired businesspeople. As well as assorted politicians, social climbers, namedroppers, and the idle rich.

Be under no illusions, moving in the same circles as businesspeople can be very helpful for building your career—you need to have a goodly number of the right sort of contacts and friends.

At the right golf club, you will rub shoulders with materially successful people who, if they are also people of honour and integrity, could become good friends, employers, employees, clients, business partners etc. Generally, this will exclude those members who are politicians, social climbers, namedroppers and the idle rich. All good.

So, learn to play golf at least tolerably well. At least well enough so you don't embarrass yourself or endanger anyone else on the course. This will require practice and probably some lessons. You don't have to become a member of a club unless you really do like the game, but it's no bad thing to be competent at the charity/client/business golf day, or when you get invited to play a round with a prospective boss, client or business associate.

There are few sports that rely as much on personal integrity as golf does. Since it is such an expansive and largely un-monitored game, it falls on the individual to be utterly honest with themselves and their fellow golfers in order to retain a fair contest in the spirit of the game. Look after your reputation on the golf course—what happens on the golf course will definitely NOT stay on the golf course. And beware of doing business or getting too close to anyone whose golf score you don't quite trust. If they cheat at golf, they probably cheat at other stuff too.

As we've already established, for the amateur hack like me the rules can be exhausting, confusing and obscure.

Fortunately, you only need to abide by six very basic rules which encapsulate all the others:

1. Dress appropriately—this shows respect for the club and for your fellow players. And, may I repeat, respect is an important trait in ALL of life.
2. "Play the ball as it lies". i.e., play the ball from the position it has come to rest in. Do not move it.

3. "Play the course as you find it". So, no breaking down branches or draining of ponds to get a clear shot back onto the fairway.
4. Use a replacement ball if you lose one or if your ball is unplayable (this will cost you a one-shot penalty).
5. Don't hold up the play. Pick-up your ball and walk to the next tee if you're taking too many shots.
6. Wear sunscreen. Seriously. Wear sunscreen.

Regarding skills;

1. Practice. Even get some lessons.
2. Keep your head down and follow through.
3. Keep soft hands on the club. Consciously relax that grip-of-death on the club.
4. Never give advice to any other player unless they ask for it. Never. It's really irritating. Therefore, please ignore the previous three points.

Concentrate. Play to win. But never ever throw a tantrum (or your clubs) after a bad shot. Remember, every shot in golf will make somebody happy. If it's not you, it will certainly be your opponent. So, chill a bit. Show them you are a good sport and control yourself.

As in life in general, if you can, avoid playing with any of the following people:

1. Yobs who think that it's all a loud joke. Golf is a game for people with manners and respect.
2. Prigs who are annoyingly fastidious about the most obscure rules and etiquette. Life's too short right?
3. Cheats.
4. Snobs.

Finally, you may need a few jokes to ease the tension during your round or to lighten the mood at the 19th hole (aka the clubhouse bar). Here are some old favourites:

Two golfers are ready to play on the 11th tee as a funeral cortege passes by. The first player stops, doffs his cap, and bows his head as the cortege passes.

"That was a really nice thing to do," the second golfer says. "It's good to see there is still some respect in the world."

"Well, it's only right," the first golfer replies. "I was married to her for 35 years."

—

After a particularly poor round, a golfer spotted a lake as she walked despondently up the 18th.

She looked at her caddie and said, "I've played so badly all day, I think I'm going to drown myself in that lake."

The caddie, quick as a flash, replied, "I'm not sure you could keep your head down that long."

—

Two golfing buddies are on the fairway approaching the 18th green. One of them is taking forever to settle into his stance over the ball. Eventually his friend asks him in exasperation, "what's taking you so long?!"

"Well" he replies, "my wife is watching from the club house terrace and I want to hit a perfect shot."

His friend gazes at the club house for a long moment, and then says "Nah, you'll never hit her from here".

—

And finally, an innocent question which is sure to put your better skilled opponent off his game and give you a small advantage. Ask him on the first tee: "So do you breathe in just before you hit your drive? Or just after?"

It's bound to play on his mind and cause havoc with his drive as he tries to figure it out on every tee shot.

—

So that's the *rapport* side of sport.

Now here are some examples of what sport can teach us about *life*. I reckon …

Life is just a lower form of cricket

Cricket is another sport which can be completely baffling to the uninitiated (much like life really). So don't let your eyes glaze over now—cricket can teach us some important lessons that can really help a lot in life. Take courage and read on …

Basically, the game works like this:[10]

"Cricket is a game played between two teams of 11 members each. In essence, it is single combat, in which an individual batsman faces off against an individual bowler. The bowler has his entire team with him on the field to help him (they're called "fielders"). But there are only two batsmen on the field, one at each end of the pitch.

The bowler hurls the ball from one end of the pitch towards the batsman at the other end in an attempt to dismiss the batsman by hitting three sticks known as the wickets at the other end,

---

10 As explained by https://www.espncricinfo.com/story/an-explanation-of-cricket-239758

or by causing the batsman to hit the ball into the air so that a fielder can catch it before it bounces, or by inducing one of a number of other indiscretions.

The batsman attempts to defend the wickets with the bat and to score runs—the currency of the game—by striking the ball to the field boundary, or far enough from the fielders to allow the batsman to run to the other end of the pitch before the ball can be returned. At least two bowlers must take turns, from alternating ends; also, there are always two batsmen on the field, each to take a turn as required.

When all but one of the batting team have been dismissed—or after an agreed period—the teams' roles are reversed. After all the players required to bat on both sides have done so either once or twice (which can take from a few hours to five days) the total number of runs accumulated by each team determines the winner. But sometimes there isn't one."

As I said, it's all a bit baffling at first. But don't be put off. The life lessons are coming:

Personally I had an illustrious cricketing career when I was at primary school—my highest score was 5 runs, and I don't think I ever took a wicket. So okay, I was complete rubbish. But that didn't stop me from loving the game.

Cricket is one of those rare team sports (with all the fun and benefits of "team") where you are also completely on your own for large parts of the game.

Imagine you're batting, it's just you, surrounded by the enemy. They're chirping you and baiting you and taunting you and trying to put you off your game. You must shut them out of your mind, you have to learn to focus on what *you're* doing and shut out all the distractions, ignore the baiting and taunting, **you have to keep your cool if you're to succeed. And focus**. Good practice for life don't you think?

Figure 8: Fielders crowding a lone batsman like vultures. One mistake and he's gone. Imagine the pressure! *Source: Cricket Concern*

As a batsman you're also fully aware that every eye in the stadium is looking at you. You're in the spotlight and you're on your own. There's no one there to help you. And the enemy is throwing everything they can at you. And your teammates, far away where they can't help you, are relying on you. In those circumstances you're going to need some reserves of **mental toughness**—more good practice for life.

Here are some other life-lessons from cricket:

Courage

Imagine you're a batsman, and you're the last wicket standing. If you can survive, you will save your team from defeat. But you're facing a demon fast bowler who's hurling a rock-hard ball towards you at lightning speed. He's strong as an ox and he's mean. He is intent on intimidating you and physically hurting you. Your every instinct is to get off that field as quickly as possible. But instead, you stand fast. You take a blow to your ribs, and then another, and then to your gloves, and to your helmet. But you refuse to be cowed. You take the pain. In the choice between *fight* or *flight*, you choose to *fight*.

This requires not just physical courage, but mental courage as well. It takes a lot of guts to stay out in the middle when everything seems to be going against you.

Cricket teaches us that sometimes, the only way to succeed is to grit our teeth and to stand fast. Life is just the same.

Now imagine this: After all that, after taking all that pain for your team, you're *dropped* for the next game. It feels like a slap. Could you deal with that mentally? Could you gather your emotions and your confidence and pick yourself up and try to get back into the team? Without bitterness?

As I say, sport can be a cruel life coach. But you'll probably need that sort of character at some point in your life, to pick yourself up and pull yourself together and to start again. And to leave the resentment and bitterness outside.

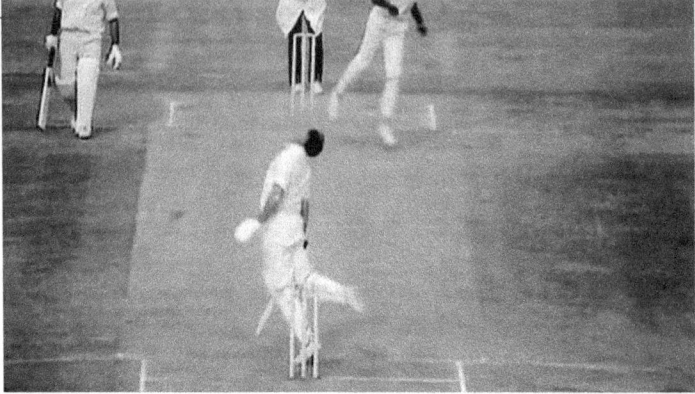

Figure 9: The BEFORE—Brian Close takes another 95-mph delivery in the ribs from the West Indian pace attack, 1976. **Source:** *The Daily Mail, UK*

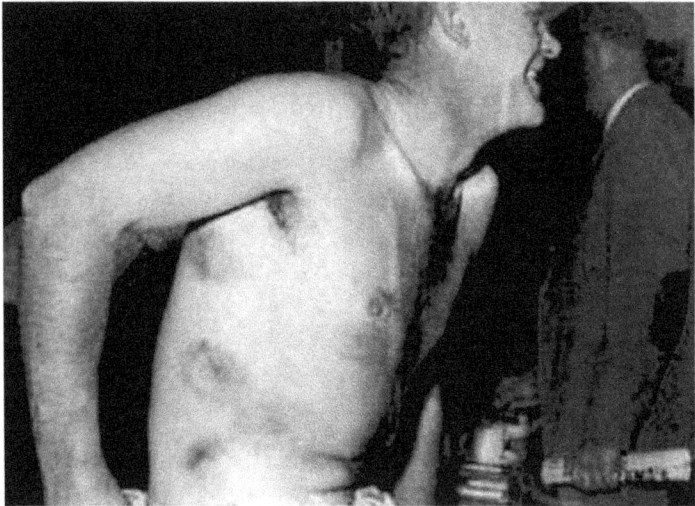

Figure 10: The AFTER—Brian Close at the end of the day's play. **Source:** *The Daily Mail, UK*

Endurance

Now imagine that you're a fast bowler, playing for your country, far away from home. It's the fifth day of the fifth test. It's been an exhausting tour. The conditions are sweltering, and after 24 days of intense cricket, your feet are blistered and bleeding, every muscle in your body is aching, the crowd is massive and against you, and the batsman is seeing the ball as if it's the size of a soccer ball. But you keep running in, keep putting your back into every delivery, keep pressing for a breakthrough. You ignore everything else, and you focus only on your next delivery. And you give it everything. Just once more.

To keep going when you are so sore and so exhausted requires not just physical endurance, but also mental endurance. It takes a lot of mental strength to keep going when everything seems to be against you.

Cricket teaches us that sometimes, success is not just about talent, but also about perseverance and determination. And life is just the same. Remember the 40% rule? Thank goodness you're tougher than you think.

Patience

This time you're a batsman: your team is under pressure to score runs to win the game. The bowler is full of guile and cunning, tempting you with swinging deliveries that are just begging to be smacked over the boundary. He's daring you to score the runs your team so desperately needs. But you know that if you miss-hit just once, you could be gone. So you resist the temptations, you watch and you wait, because you know that:

> Sometimes the best shot to play is "the leave". In the heat of the moment, it's also one of the hardest.

Playing the "leave" requires not just patience, but immense discipline as well. It takes a lot of mental strength to stay focused and to wait for the right opportunity to present itself. To not get carried away in the moment. Cricket teaches us that sometimes, the best strategy is to be patient, to protect your "wickets" and to survive a bit longer. And then to strike when the right opportunity presents itself. Life, especially in business, is just the same.

In many ways Life is like a Test Match

T20 cricket is the short format of the game where each team gets to bat for a maximum of 20 overs. The game is completed within a few hours and is fast-paced and highly entertaining. The focus is on scoring runs quickly, hitting spectacular boundaries, and taking quick, audacious singles. There are dancing cheerleaders and smoke machines and massive, loud crowds. It's wildly exciting.

In test cricket on the other hand, matches can last up to five days (and even then, still end in a draw). Test cricket is more about patience, strategy, and skill.

Now T20 can be a lot of fun as a batsman, especially when you're in a purple patch, smashing the ball to all corners of the park. You think every risk is worth taking, and that you can handle anything. But in a flash, it's over—your wickets are cartwheeling behind you from a fast in-swinger and you're done, out.

Playing T20 requires a great deal of skill and athleticism for sure. But compared to Test cricket, nowhere near the amount of endurance or mental strength. Test cricket will expose your every weakness, slowly and relentlessly. It will try to grind you down, strangle you psychologically and exhaust you physically. To win at test cricket, you need to be skilled AND have incredible mental resilience.

As with chess, in Test cricket you need to have a strategy that looks beyond just the next move. You need to have a longer-term view.

> You need to have the confidence to keep doing the right things consistently so that, even if the benefits are not immediately apparent, you don't flail about and do something wild. You stay patient because you know that when you're doing the right things, eventually the right results will come.

Life is just the same.

I've often found it useful to remind myself that in many areas of life: building a career, your marriage, raising children, growing a business, investing, it's much more about the long game, about doing the rights things consistently, than about short-term bursts of brilliance. It takes time for the compounding effects to kick-in. That's why, generally, building something of value takes time and care and sustained effort.

In my experience, much of life is very much like Test cricket. It's quite simply not a T20 game.

What sport is Not

So maybe a last word on sport … or to be more precise, on what sport is NOT.

Sport is NOT an opportunity for you to rehash your own sporting dreams through your child. We've all seen those parents next to the football pitch screaming at their kids to do this, run there, mark-that player, get up, come ON!!! Blah blah blah.

Some go even further, they shout at the ref, verbally abuse the opposition and complain to the coach when their kid isn't selected for the A-team.

Don't be that guy. Seriously.

Those guys are an embarrassment to their kids and an embarrassment to themselves. And guaranteed, their kid will stop playing sport as soon as they're allowed to.

A mate of mine once told me the most incredible story about a friend of his. This bloke had been a keen cricket player as a kid but (like me) was frankly pretty rubbish at it. Never-the-less he loved it, and his dad was always very supportive. When the kid was disappointed that he'd only scored 8 runs, his dad's response would be "but what a classy 8 that was!". Well, this bloke never lost his love for the game, but he also never progressed very far. No matter, his dad kept encouraging and supporting. Never being pushy. Never being harsh. Never being disappointed in him. Just being encouraging.

It was only years later, as an adult, that this bloke came to learn that his dad had played cricket for England. Yet had never told him.

You see, his dad knew it was no longer about himself. His time had come and gone. Now it was about his son. And he knew that his responsibility as a dad was to nurture confidence and the love of the game in his son's heart. Not shame and anxiety and embarrassment.

I've never forgotten that story. I hope you get the point.

What an example. What a dad!

16

ABOUT YOUR CAREER

In many ways your career will end up defining you. It doesn't determine who you *are*, as a person I mean, but it will certainly define a lot in your life. Here's the thing: you're likely to spend about forty years of your life at it. If it fulfils you, you will be fulfilled. If it drains you, you will wither. Your progress in it will influence your level of self-confidence. It will determine where you live and how you live. It will determine what type of holidays you can afford. It may affect your health and sense of wellbeing. And it will determine the security and quality of your retirement. So best you take it seriously.

What's a career?

You need to regularly reflect on the health and direction of your career, and if it's going where you want it to go, at the pace you want it to go at. And if not, you should consider some adjustments (we spoke about this in the chapter on making a Life Plan).

And by "career" I don't mean "job"—your career is much bigger than your job, it's the summation of all your experience and the trajectory of that experience. For example, let's say you're an electrician. Your job is wiring houses and doing that really well. But your career will encompass wiring houses, working in a team, leading a team, learning about marketing and costing and business development and handling customers and project management and ordering materials and cashflow and starting a business and running a business and managing people and accounts and taxes and saving and investing and growing the business and buying and selling businesses and starting a trust fund. The sum of all that is your career. You get the picture?

I also don't mean to suggest that your career should be solely focused on the accumulation of wealth. Doing stuff that you enjoy, that fulfils you and gives you purpose is super important. But I am saying that your career needs to grow and expand so that you can grow and expand intellectually and as a person. Be ambitious about improving yourself and expanding your horizons. Aim to be more next year than what you are now.

But maybe you're one of those (actually, I mean "us") who aren't exactly sure what they want to do with their lives …

It'll come to you

———— **"** ————

"Don't feel guilty if you don't know what
you want to do with your life;
The most interesting people I know,
Didn't know at 22 what they wanted to do with their lives,
Some of the most interesting 40-year-olds I know still don't".

—BAZ LUHRMANN, EVERYBODY'S FREE (THE SUNSCREEN SONG)

The reality is that there are very few people who know when they're twenty what they will still enjoy doing in another five years, let alone another forty. The good news is that you really don't need to. *It'll come to you.* You just need to do whatever is in front of you today. And to do it to the best of your ability, with a view to gleaning as much higher-level knowledge from the task as possible—knowledge that you can apply to a broader and broader field. Take the electrician in the example above: over the course of his career was he primarily an electrician or a marketer or a business manager or an entrepreneur or all of the above? Looking back, he didn't need to worry about whether he would enjoy being an electrician for the rest of their days. All he had to worry about was being a good electrician *today,* with a view to gleaning as much higher-level knowledge from the task as possible—knowledge that he could apply to a successively broader and higher field. Or use to pivot to a different field.

I can really relate to this. I happened to study engineering at university. I don't really know why. My parents said it was a good idea and I didn't know any different. Anyway, for quite a few years I was fully focused on being the best engineer that I could be. And I really enjoyed it. Now, after thirty years, I find that I am far more interested in the actual *business* side of engineer-

WATCH THIS ...

pple founder, Steve Jobs' famous speech at Stanford University.

*https://youtu.be/UF8uR6Z-6KLc?si=N6-NUag-GOI_8kK_*

ing and in *people* and in *finance.* Engineering is still my springboard, but apart from knowing the right questions to ask and applying some engineering experience, I do very little actual engineering. I'd prefer to employ bright engineers and concentrate on growing great teams and great businesses—it's completely different to what I was doing when I started.

—— 66 ——

"Do what you can, with what you have, where you are."

—THEODORE ROOSEVELT

Cool. But that said, irrespective where you start or where you are now, you still need to …

Take ownership

As I've said before, we work for three reasons: to earn, to learn and to have fun. And if any one of these is deficient for too long, then that's a red flag for your career, and you need to consider some changes.

The good news is that in many ways, control of these three things lies in *your own hands*. Unfortunately, most people just don't see the possibilities all around them. And most people are not sufficiently intentional about building and developing their careers.

Firstly, *they're not serious enough about learning new and deeper and broader skills, or gaining deeper, broader, and better experience.* And so, after a while, their careers plateau—they reach a certain level, and they get stuck there.

Secondly, *they don't really understand the nature of money.* The money you earn is nothing else than the measure of the value you create for *other* people. Therefore, if you want to make more money you need to start by asking yourself "How can I create more value?" And how do you create value? By solving problems for other people and giving other people what they want. Luckily people want a billion different things: your boss wants you to do your job faster, more accurately, with less supervision, with more of your heart and brain involved. Other people want more time, cool holidays, entertainment, fun, adventure, more sleep, less pain, to be fit, to be thinner, to be attractive, cars, houses, food, fuel, transport, their lawns mowed and so on and so on. And guess what, if you can provide some of these solutions for them, they'll pay you money in exchange.

> *This is a big aha moment*: *If you want to make serious money you can't act like the world owes you a living.* Instead, you have to identify which group of people you're going to create value for and then you have to create as much value for them as possible so they will keep coming back to you and keep paying you for the value exchange.

Thirdly, *you need to understand the importance of marketing.* Marketing is simply the process of communicating the benefits of your value solutions to your target market. Marketing is a big topic on its own, and know this, if you're an employee, your "target market" includes your boss. You need to ensure that he/she sees the value you are creating.

The sweetest words a boss can ever hear is: "I've done what you asked me to do, But I think it would be even better if I also did this and that and this other thing. And by the way, what's next? I want to do more. I've been thinking about how we can do this better/faster/cheaper. I've been thinking of how we can grow the business, what if …."

Think and speak like that to your boss and you're already on the road to bigger things.

The kiss of death to career advancement is telling a boss "Sorry, I can't do that—it's not in my job description". Or, when you get asked to do that extra thing, "Sure, how much extra will I get paid?" If that's your attitude, you've already reached the top in your career. Sorry. Red Pill.

——— 66 ———

*Your attitude, not your aptitude, will
determine your altitude.*

—ZIG ZIGLAR

Be intentional about developing your career

While many people are content to land a job in their field and then let time and luck dictate their career path, there are definite advantages to grabbing the bull by the horns and taking proactive steps to plan your career path. The process is exactly analogous the Life Plan we discussed in Chapter 11, but more focused on *the tools required* to attain your career goals.

———— 66 ————

"Most people over-estimate what they can accomplish in a
year, and underestimate what they can accomplish in five."

—BILL GATES

So have a 5-year career plan. Write it down.

Make sure that you focus on each of the following:

1. Invest in yourself
Seek out continuing and professional education programs to refresh
your skills or add new skills to your repertoire. Adding new skills to
a growing base of good experience hugely increases your value to the
business fraternity. The more you learn, the more you earn. Quality
bubbles to the top. It always does.

2. Get a professional designation
Many industries have professional bodies that regulate professionals
working in the field. In some fields (like medicine and engineering
and boxing), certification is a precondition of working in the field. In
others, it signals that you are well-trained and competent and it gives
you credibility in the marketplace.

3. Develop your soft skills
It goes without saying that technical competence to execute your role
is a prerequisite for any career, but soft skills such as communication, teamwork, critical thinking/problem-solving, professionalism/
work ethic, leadership, EQ etc are the jet-fuel which will propel your
progress.

I can't emphasise the importance of these skills enough. Ultimately
they *WILL* determine your career trajectory. Develop your soft skills
by looking for courses and professional development opportunities.
Read.

4. Build your network

Don't underestimate the power of making meaningful professional connections. While some might roll their eyes, the simple fact is that who you know is at least as important as what you know. There are many ways to do this. Join the professional association in your field, attend their events, sit on their committees, become a speaker at their conferences.

5. Every year or so, deeply consider your career path

About once a year, you should go out and refresh your network, check out new opportunities and assess the trajectory of your career. Keep abreast of new industry trends to remain competitive in the job market if you should ever choose (or need) to leave your current workplace, or if you want to start your own business.

6. Search for the value in feedback or criticism

Each piece of feedback you receive can be used to help you grow and further develop in your career. Try not to focus on the method of delivery or the person providing you with the feedback. Instead, you should do your best to avoid getting upset and take the value out of the message you are receiving and move on.

Remember: Pain + Reflection = Progress

7. Be reliable

It is essential that you match your words with your actions. We all appreciate people we can trust and depend on. Bosses are no different. If you tell your boss you can finish a project by a certain date, then you should take the necessary steps to finish the project accordingly. Relationships are essential to any business, and without trust, a relationship cannot be cultivated.

8. Ask important questions

Successful professionals ask important questions. Asking questions will build your knowledge and contribute to your learning process and development. You should also ask questions about things that are not directly related to your job title—this indicates that you are a broad thinker and will help you gain a better understanding of the organization as a whole.

9. Don't be afraid to speak up

Meetings are meant for team members to share their thoughts and ideas on important topics that affect the business. If you have an idea or if you have a reason to believe an idea shouldn't be implemented, then you should mention it in a professional way with accurate data to back up your claims. Request a face-to-face meeting with a supervisor if you need to discuss a sensitive matter or ask for advice.

10. Develop your personal brand

We've discussed this before in Chapter 13. Don't under-estimate the impact of your personal brand on your career trajectory.

11. Be quietly confident

Confidence leads to productivity at work. It is important to develop your confidence to effectively communicate your ideas and to demonstrate leadership. But stay humble—always remember that you will gain the most by being affable and respected, rather than arrogant and resented.

12. Be a team player

Working with a team and collaborating with other employees is a central part of most jobs. Do your best to work with the team instead of against the team. Many great things can be accomplished by working well with your teammates and often it is essential for the success of a business, as well as your route to recognition and progress.

13. Learn to Delegate

The art of delegation is a critical factor in effective leadership. But unfortunately, a huge proportion of "leaders" have no idea what it entails or how important it is. Poor delegators end up becoming a bottle-neck to productivity, constricting it, rather than accelerating it.

> **The golden rule of delegation** is to delegate tasks or responsibilities to others in a way that sets clear expectations (including quality, budget and timeline), provides sufficient resources and support, and allows for feedback and accountability. Then allow them to get on with it. Do NOT micro-manage. "Empowerment with accountability", that's the recipe.

What employers want

Maybe a few thoughts on what (wise) employers look for in prospective employees:

It's quite simple really, and it comes down to the **Three C's: Character, Competence and Chemistry**.[11] In that order of importance.

CHARACTER encompasses things like having personal integrity, valuing truth and honesty, humility, teachability, being reliable, someone who exhibits positive intent for colleagues, the business, customers and suppliers. No malicious blaming, no complaining, no shaming. Do you take *personal ownership* to ensure successful outcomes or do you ride on the backs of others? Do you persevere, or do you quit easily?

Character is by far the most important of the Three C's—it's the one thing that you either have or you haven't. It's hard to assess in an interview but be sure that it will be on the checklist when they check your social media trail and speak to your references and put you through

---

11   The Three C's were first articulated by Bill Hybels in his book Leadership Axioms. It's well worth a read.

the psychometric tests. *Doubts about character = no hire. Simple as that. Red Pill.*

COMPETENCE is probably the easiest one to assess—does this person have the right qualifications (from well branded, reputable institutions), and the right experience (from well branded, reputable institutions)? It's mostly "yes" or "no" and it's determined initially on the basis of your CV. The quality of your qualifications and your experience get you the interview.

Then, in the interview they'd like to get a feel for your intelligence—not as measured by your grades, but by your ability to *think*. The level of questions that you ask. How curious you are, not about how much leave you'll be entitled to, but about challenges, opportunities, aspirations for the team and for the company.

If they get the strong feeling that, even though your current qualifications are not the highest, but your *intelligence*, your *mind* set, your *attitude* sets you apart; then that's cool—competence can be learned. And they'll be happy to proceed.

CHEMISTRY refers to "fit". Does this person fit into the existing team / corporate culture or (if that is what is required), will this person be a disruptor? Chemistry includes ideas like "influence"—is this person likely to be a positive influence for progress in the team, or a negative influence, or no influence at all? Potential leaders are natural attractors, they are effortless influencers. What is their EQ like? Do they genuinely care for people? Or view them as just a means to an end? They also look for action-orientated people who are comfortable taking initiative.

> Good leaders at any level make things happen.

These three attributes are super important. You need to think about them carefully when applying for a new position, or when you're hiring.

READ THIS ...

Courageous Leadership: Field-tested strategy for the 360° Leader by Bill Hybels. This book is one of the best books on leadership I've ever read. It's crisp, simple and easy to read. Start with this one.

Leadership Axioms by Bill Hybels. Another great but easy read on Leadership with plenty of practical tips that you can start applying immediately.

The morality of money

As you may have noticed, I consider that money is quite an important part of life. I've seen plenty of hardship and sadness when money gets tight:

Recently a friend of mine related a story of when he was a young school principal and was forced to call a single mom into his office to discuss long overdue school fees. She arrived in a long overcoat and after a few minutes of heart-breaking details about her dire financial situation, she looked at him with tears in her eyes and asked if there was perhaps another way in which she could pay the debt. And she opened her coat.

Can you imagine that? Can you imagine how desperate that poor woman was to be willing to offer herself up and humiliate herself in that way? Believe me, it's not that uncommon.

I've also seen plenty of reckless spending by people who can't afford the lifestyles they lead; they think it's important to project an image of success and so they choose debt over savings. They are financially illiterate and they repeatedly make financial decisions which ultimately condemn them and their children to hardship and worry.

I'll say it again, money is not the most important thing in life. But it's pretty close. When you need it, you really do need it. So take it seriously. And take building your career seriously.

> **But here's the thing:** with money comes responsibility. The morality of money is an issue that you should consider deeply.

How you make it, and *how* and *what* you spend it on are important reflections of your personal values.

Therefore, develop a perspective which recognises that whatever wealth you may have and even your means to accumulate that wealth (like your hands and eyes, your intellect and skills) are all gifts from God.

Cultivate a mindset which emphasizes the importance of integrity and balance in accumulation, as well as wise stewardship and generosity, and be serious about using your wealth for a greater good than just for your own benefit. One day, like it or not, you will be called to account for the way in which you used the money that God gifted to you in this life.

And finally

Remember, no one on their deathbed ever wished they'd spent more time working late at the office. ***Your family needs you to be present.*** Read that last sentence again. Underline it. Don't forget it. *Quality* is not a substitute for *quantity* when it comes to time spent with your kids. They need both.

17

DOING YOUR OWN THING

At heart, I guess I'm a corporate animal, with an entrepreneurial bent. I've been in both worlds, and I know that making your way in the corporate world is not every one's idea of a fulfilling life. That said, it does have some upsides—structure, and discipline, and colleagues, and brand, and customers, and capital and so on. For me, I like nothing better than the freedom to be an entrepreneur *within* a business and to grow that business and the people in it. On the other hand, there is definitely something very thrilling about doing your own thing, on your own terms and chasing your own dreams.

You're thinking anyway, so why not think bigger?

Let's start with some basics about maximising your income …

1. Business *owners* generally earn more that their *employees*. Duh.
2. Therefore, ownership is generally a better route to prosperity than employment.
3. Therefore, if you work for a corporate, you should ultimately aspire to the Executive Level, with share options (which = ownership + employment).
4. OR you need to aspire to, at some point, becoming the owner of your *own business* or a partner in a business.
5. There are only so many hours in a day. So, selling time (charging by the hour, as some doctors, lawyers and consultants do) has a natural and very rigid earnings cap—no matter what you do, you can't make more hours in the day. Therefore, maximising

your income if you charge by the hour means that either you need to also take a cut from what other more junior people in the company sell their time at (the partners in consulting companies do this), or you need to increase your charge-out rate. And that is only possible if you become more highly expert and sought after for which you're going to need to continually invest in growing your expertise AND growing your personal brand value (viz marketing yourself).

Alternatively (or, in addition), you could *sell a product* where the number of products that can be sold depends only on what can be manufactured and what the market will take. It's far easier to procure more gizmos to sell than it is to procure more hours in the day.

Therefore, try to also sell a product, or someone else's time, not only your own time.

For the Virgin Entrepreneur

If you're in a 9-to-5 and the call of the wild, free, exhilarating world of the entrepreneur is calling, then all strength to you. We're going to talk about some great strategies to help you succeed in just a minute. But before we do that, may I just remind you of the **1st law of Wing Walking** (Chapter 7):

——— **66** ———

"Never let go of what you've got until you've got a firm hold of something else".

Let's just unpack that a little further in the context of starting your own business:

The first decision you're likely to face as a first-time entrepreneur is whether you should quit your day job and go all-in on starting a business. There are two options:

Option 1: Follow your passion, quit your job and jump off the deep end. After all, choosing not to go all-in implies a lack of belief and commitment. And if you don't have that, you'll never make it right? Stirring stuff.

Option 2: Keep your day job for as long as possible. First prove that your idea for a business actually works. Prove you can make money. Prove you're willing to spend nights and weekends on your startup. Prove (mainly to yourself) you're not just running away from a job you don't like, rather than towards the business you feel compelled to start.

Option 2 probably sounds a bit "*meh*". But here's why it's almost always the correct one:

> You need to preserve your power to say "no".

Unless you're still living with your parents or you have a spouse earning enough to keep house and home together, you're going to need money. And if you quit your day job too soon, before your new venture has sufficient free cash-flow, you're going to have to make decisions you wouldn't otherwise make in order to make that money.

Desperation limits your options and almost always leads to sub-optimal choices. When you need to put food on the table and pay the rent and keep the kids in school, you'll take clients you know you shouldn't, clients that are bad payers or who are never satisfied, who will cost you more—in time, effort and resources—than they are worth. You'll cut margins to levels you know you shouldn't and then struggle to raise prices later. You'll hire employees you know you shouldn't and inevitably suffer the consequences. You'll take on any old investor and sacrifice more of your equity than you'd like. Or worse, you'll sink into debt and a whole lot of stress.

All of this you'll do. You'll hate to do it, but because money is so tight, you'll have no options.

Keeping your day job preserves your power to say no to sub-optimal decisions and buys you the time required to get things right: Your prototype isn't ready? No problem, you'll have time to keep improving it. The supplier you found isn't performing? You'll have time to find another.

When money is tight, options shrink. And so does the quality of the choices you can make.

Therefore, almost always, keeping your day job for as long as possible is the wise approach for first-time business owners. It's also the hardest: sacrifice, discipline and massive amounts of after-hours hard work will be required. But these are all part of the selection process: If you aren't willing to work hard and sacrifice, your new business will probably fail whether you keep your day job or not. And especially if you don't preserve your power to say no to things that decrease the odds of success.

Red Pill time, you need to think about this stuff.

All of that said, starting your own business can be a thrilling and very rewarding experience. With the right mindset, tools, and strategies, and a bit of good advice from those who've been there and done that; there's no reason for you not to become a huge success.

Minimise your Risk: Maximise your Chances

Now, because we like to *make good decisions consistently* (remember Chapter 1), let's start by discussing three practical ways to become an entrepreneur whilst *minimising your risk and maximising your chances*:

No matter how brilliant you think your business idea might be, it's very hard to come up with completely new products and business models and customers simultaneously, all from scratch and hit the jackpot from the get-go. In fact, it's so hard that the vast majority of start-ups that try things this way round end up failing within a year. That doesn't need to be you.

Generally, it's far better, especially if it's your first venture, to either:

1. Imitate other successful businesses and strategies

Imitation is a powerful tool that can help you minimise risk when starting a business. Many successful entrepreneurs have started their businesses by imitating other successful businesses or strategies. The key here is to identify successful businesses in your industry or niche and study what they do to achieve their success. Look at their products, marketing strategies, customer service, pricing models, and more. Ask yourself, what are they doing right that you can do too? What mistakes have they made that you can avoid?

Imitation doesn't mean copying or stealing someone's intellectual property. Instead, it means adapting and applying successful strategies to your own business in a way that suits your unique circumstances. For example, if you are starting a restaurant, you could look at successful restaurants in your area and see what they offer that customers love. Then, you could apply those features to your own restaurant in a way that aligns with your brand and vision.

2. Buy a franchise

Another way to minimise risk when starting a business is to become a franchisee. A franchise is a business model in which an entrepreneur buys the right to use an existing brand, products, and systems from a franchisor. Franchising offers several advantages to entrepreneurs, such as:

- **Established brand recognition and reputation:** As a franchisee, you don't have to start from scratch to establish your brand. The franchisor has already done the hard work of creating a recognised and respected brand.
- **Proven business model:** The franchisor has already tested the business model and knows what works and what doesn't. This can save you a lot of time and money that you would otherwise spend on trial and error.

- **Training and support:** The franchisor provides training and support to franchisees to ensure that they understand how to run the business and adhere to the standards set by the franchisor.

While franchising offers many benefits, it's essential to do your due diligence before signing a franchise agreement. You need to understand the terms of the agreement, the initial and ongoing fees, the support you will receive from the franchisor, and the rights and responsibilities of both parties.

3. Buy an existing business

Buying an existing business is another way to minimise risk when starting a business. When you buy an existing business, you acquire an established customer base, a proven business model, and an existing revenue stream. This can save you a lot of time and money that you would otherwise spend on building a new business from scratch. However, buying an existing business requires careful research and due diligence to ensure that you are making a sound investment.

Here are some things to consider when buying an existing business:

- **Financials:** Review the financial statements of the business to understand its revenue, profit, and cash flow. Look for any red flags such as declining revenue or profitability, outstanding debts, or pending lawsuits. Ask an accountant to help you with this.
- **Operations:** Understand how the business operates, its products or services, suppliers, employees, and customers. Identify any operational challenges that you may face and how you plan to address them.
- **Industry:** Research the industry in which the business operates, its competitors, market trends, and growth potential. Identify opportunities for growth and expansion.
- **Legal:** Review any contracts, leases, licenses, permits, or other legal documents related to the business

Cool, so three good strategies to begin with PLUS the 1st Law of Wing-walking! You're off to a great start.

Now let's take a look at the other end of the scale—the *three worst things to do when becoming an entrepreneur.* I've included these because you'll be aghast at how often people (like me) have done them, and then wondered why things didn't work out so swimmingly well:

1. Invest too much money upfront

One of the biggest mistakes new entrepreneurs make is investing too much money upfront without fully testing their business idea or market. It's important to *start small and gradually scale up* as you learn more about your target market and how your business can serve their needs.

2. Ignore market research

Many new entrepreneurs fall in love with their business idea and assume that others will too. However, it's important to do your due diligence and conduct market research to understand if there's actually a demand for your product or service. Without this information, you may end up investing time and money in a business that doesn't have a viable market.

I fell into this trap myself once: I started a business based on a "brilliant" new design for an engineering product. I got venture capital funding, registered patents, optimised the manufacturing process, even installed some prototypes which performed famously. All good. It was a great product. But I had failed to understand a key client requirement: "Who do we sue if this thing goes wrong?". I was a tiny start-up, and as much as the clients liked the product, they needed to purchase from someone with balance sheet, someone they could sue if things went wrong. It would have been far better for me to have gone to a large corporate in the same field and offer to develop the product under their auspices and brand on the basis of profit share or as a joint venture. By the time I realised this, the big players had caught up and I had run out of money. Lesson learned. Scar earned.

1. Failing to create a solid business plan

A business plan is essential for any new entrepreneur. It outlines your goals, target market, competition, financial projections, and more. Without a business plan, it's difficult to stay on track and make informed decisions. A solid plan will also help you secure funding and investors, so take the time to create one before launching your business.

READ THIS ...

Good to Great: Why Some Companies Make the Leap ... and Others Don't by Jim Collins—A classic business book that examines why some companies succeed while others fail, and what makes the difference. The book provides practical insights for entrepreneurs looking to build great businesses.

The Lean Entrepreneur: How Visionaries Create Products, Innovate with New Ventures, and Disrupt Markets by Brant Cooper and Patrick Vlaskovits. This book provides a framework for entrepreneurs to build successful businesses by focusing on the most critical tasks, while ignoring the rest. It provides practical tips and tools to help entrepreneurs achieve more with less effort.

The Laptop Lifestyle

The ability to work from anywhere at anytime, using just a laptop and an internet connection, is a super attractive lifestyle. It's very suited to entrepreneurship and it's really doable. Cool!

Again, because we like to *make good decisions consistently*, let's follow the cautious approach …

Starting a side hustle, where you don't immediately leave your day-job but instead slowly grow an income on the side, is a great segway into the laptop lifestyle. There are many different types of side hustles (visit **www.sidehustlestack.co** or **https://sidehusl.com** which list lots of options), and here are some examples that might pique your interest:[12]

1. Get paid to read and review books online

Could anything be easier? Go to **https://onlinebookclub.org**, read books and write reviews. You get paid per review. And there are other similar sites out there.

2. Get paid to take online marketing surveys

Another easy one, visit **www.surveyjunkie.com**. Or search for others like it.

3. Online tutoring

With the growing demand for online education, tutoring has become a popular side hustle. You can offer your services on platforms such as **https://tutorme.com** or **https://www.chegg.com/uversity**. Tutoring can be done in a variety of subjects, such as mathematics, science, English, or even coding. The best part is that you can do it from the comfort of your own home and set your own schedule.

---

12 A word to the wise—have your radar up about any and all online opportunities, there are plenty of scam artists out there. So be alert, do your homework, and do some background checks on all these sites.

4. Freelance writing

If you have a way with words and enjoy writing, freelance writing can be a great side hustle. There are many online platforms such as **https://www.upwork.com** and **https://www.fiverr.com** where you can find writing gigs, or you can reach out to businesses and blogs directly. You can write anything from blog posts and articles to product descriptions and social media content. The earning potential is quite high, and you can do it from anywhere.

5. Selling products online

Selling products online is another great way to make money on the side. With the rise of e-commerce platforms like **Amazon (https://affiliate-program.amazon.com)** and **Etsy (https://www.etsy.com/affiliates)**, it has never been easier to start your own online store. You can sell anything from handmade crafts to digital products, and you don't need to invest a lot of money to get started. You can also use social media platforms like **Instagram** and **Facebook** to reach more customers.

Here is a basic overview of the process:

- **Sign up for an account**
  To start selling on Amazon or Etsy, you will need to create an account. This will require some basic information such as your name, address, and payment details. You will also need to choose a seller name and set up your profile.

- **Create a listing**
  Once your account is set up, you can start creating your product listings. You will need to provide a title, description, and images of your products, as well as set a price. Be sure to include all relevant information about your product, such as size, colour, and materials used.

- **Price your product**
  Pricing your product correctly is key to making a profit. Be sure to

research the prices of similar products on the platform and factor in the cost of production and shipping.

- **Fulfil orders**
  Once your product is listed, you can start receiving orders. Be sure to keep track of your inventory and fulfil orders promptly. Both Amazon and Etsy have a built-in system for tracking and fulfilling orders.

- **Shipping and handling**
  You will need to handle the shipping and handling of your orders. This can be done through a third-party shipping service, or you can use the fulfilment services offered by Amazon or Etsy.

- **Monitor and Optimize**
  Regularly check your sales and customer reviews, see which product is doing well and which is not. Optimize your listing and pricing accordingly.

Smart Hack: Find cool products that are selling well on other websites. Select those that are great sellers AND where deliver is free. Then just add them to your own product listing. When someone orders from you. You place an order on the original supplier, using your customers delivery address. You charge your customer the original price plus a mark-up and the delivery is taken care of without you lifting a finger. Neat huh. ☺

These are just a few examples of great side hustles that can help you to augment your income. The key is to find something you enjoy and are good at, and then put in the effort to make it a success. With a little bit of hard work and determination, you can turn your side hustle into a full-time business.

Affiliate Programs

Affiliate programs have become increasingly popular in recent years as a way for individuals and businesses to earn money online. These programs allow you to promote products or services from *other* companies and to earn a commission for every sale that is made through their unique referral link. The concept of affiliate marketing is not new, but with the rise of e-commerce and the internet, it has become a viable way for people to make money from anywhere, including from a laptop lifestyle.

One of the benefits of affiliate marketing is that it is relatively low-cost to start. Unlike traditional businesses, which often require significant investments in inventory, equipment, and other resources, affiliate marketing can be done with just a computer and an internet connection. This makes it an attractive option for those looking to start a business on a budget.

One of the key strategies for success in affiliate marketing is to find a niche that you are passionate about. This will not only make it more enjoyable for you to work in but also make it easier for you to identify and promote products that will be of interest to your target audience.

There are many online tools that can be used to start an affiliate marketing business. Some of the most popular include:

1. Affiliate Networks:

These are platforms that connect merchants with affiliate marketers. Some popular affiliate networks include **Commission Junction, ClickBank**, and **Amazon Associates**.

2. Link Tracking and Management Tools:

These tools allow you to track clicks on your affiliate links, so you can see which links are performing well and which are not. Some popular link tracking tools include **LinkTrackr** and **ClickMeter.**

3. Analytics and Reporting Tools:

And don't forget the importance of tracking and analysing your results—treat it like the real business it is afterall! This will allow you to see which products and strategies are working and which are not, so you can make adjustments and optimize your efforts. These tools allow you to track your website's traffic and performance, so you can see which pages and products are performing well and which are not. Some popular analytics and reporting tools include **Google Analytics** and **Google Search Console.**

4. Email Marketing Tools:

These tools allow you to send promotional emails to your audience, which can be a great way to drive sales. Some popular email marketing tools include **Mailchimp** and **Aweber.**

5. Social Media Management Tools:

These tools allow you to schedule and post content to your social media accounts, which can be a great way to promote your affiliate products. Some popular social media management tools include **Hootsuite** and **Buffer.**

6. Content Creation Tools:

These tools allow you to create content such as blog posts, videos and podcasts, which can be a great way to attract an audience and promote your affiliate products. Some popular content creation tools include **Canva**, **Adobe Premiere Pro** and **Audacity**.

It's worth noting that not all tools are necessary for every affiliate marketer, so see what suits your needs and budget and start from there.

And a last thought, be very careful about what you post online (remember your BRAND, chapter 13). That video or opinion that may seem so cool, or funny or clever when you're twenty may be properly cringe-worthy a few years later when your boss sees it, or your children, or your mother.

READ THIS ...

The Laptop Millionaire: How Anyone Can Escape the 9 to 5 and Make Money Online by Mark Anastasi. This book provides easy to follow step-by-step strategies you can use to make money online.

18

MASTERY OR COMPETENCE

There's something about most of us that always seeks the easier, quicker, less onerous route to a desired outcome. I suppose in a way that can be a good thing—if you combine intelligence and inventiveness with just the right amount of laziness, you're bound to find a more efficient solution to many tasks. In fact, even Bill Gates thinks you should actually hire lazy people. Seriously. He famously said, "I choose a lazy person to do a hard job. Because a lazy person will find an easy way to do it." Now, Uncle Bill wasn't talking about lying-in-bed-all-day-while-watching-Tik-Toc laziness; Gates was talking about *efficiency*. He was talking about proactively working *smarter*, not *harder*.

That's the right kind of lazy—the one that finds the quickest, simplest way to accomplish stuff.

On the other hand, life has taught me that where there is little effort, there is generally little result. And, unfortunately, great results invariably require a great deal of effort. And time.

That said, we need to distinguish between wanting to be highly competent and being a master. Lets' start with being a master:

There are no short cuts to mastery

Robert Greene, author of the bestselling book, *Mastery*, said "The very desire to find shortcuts makes you eminently unsuited for any kind of mastery. There is no possible reversal to this process." Mastery takes "tenacious effort". And it takes *intensity*. Sorry, it's Red Pill time again.

In the same vein, you've probably heard of the 10,000-hour rule, which was popularized by Malcolm Gladwell in his book *Outliers*. As Gladwell tells it, it typically takes at least 10,000 hours of intensive work to achieve mastery of complex skills or advanced concepts. Like playing football *at the highest level*, or the guitar, or computer programming or understanding economics.

READ THIS ...

Mastery by Robert Greene. Greene mines the biographies of great historical figures for the common ingredients required to become a "master" in any field. He demonstrates how humans are hardwired for achievement – it's a canny and erudite explanation of just what it takes to be great.

Outliers by Malcolm Gladwell. This brilliant and entertaining book investigates what sets high achievers apart - from Bill Gates to the Beatles. Gladwell asks the question: What makes high-achievers different? The answers may surprise you.

Gladwell described one case study, about which he wrote: "their research suggests that once a musician has enough ability to get into a top music school, the thing that distinguishes one performer from another is how hard he or she works. That's it."

Of course, plain hard work in your chosen field is not *all* there is to "it". Things like having good teachers and genes (if you're an athlete) and opportunities are also important. But the point is this: mastery of anything takes a *lot of time* and a *lot of effort*. And there is no way around that.

This has two important implications:

1. **If you want to become a world master at something, be it music or sport or your profession, you're probably going to need to change the way you live your life**. Say what?! Yep, you're going to need to frankly assess your life and honestly answer the question: "Am I living a lifestyle that can reasonably result in me becoming a master at this thing?" Do I really practice long enough and intensely enough to become world class at this? Have I got the right coach or mentor? Am I being stretched a bit more every day? Do I train hard enough? Am I serious enough about my health and diet?

   If not, you must be prepared to change. As Stephen Covey said: "*Your systems are perfectly designed to get the results that you are getting*". So, if the trajectory of your performance isn't taking you towards your goals, you must change your system. And that means how you live your life. You up for that?

2. **You're going to need time.** Don't let your ambition lie to you and tell you that you should be CEO of the company when you're three years out of university. Or that you should be promoted now because you're bright and have incredible potential. These attributes may be prerequisites to ultimate achievement but without the required *experience* you will be setting yourself up for failure. Say you work at developing your skills for eight hours every workday, then 10,000 hours equates to about five years! And that's if you do nothing else except hone these specific skills for eight diligent, intense hours every day! Maybe in reality it's more like ten years!

Let's call this your apprentice period—it's a necessity, the need and value of which should never be underestimated. It's the foundation of enduring mastery and competence. Unfortunately, twenty years of experience generally takes twenty years to get. You want to set someone up for failure?—promote them too soon.

So, allow yourself the time required to become truly proficient—don't be conned into skipping steps to shorten the journey or become discouraged by comparing yourself to others. Ultimately, true quality bubbles to the top. Always. But it takes time.

That said, it's also important to draw the distinction between getting five years of experience or one year of experience five times. If you're not progressing in your job (learning more, faster, on a broader base, taking on more and more responsibility), then you're stagnating and it's time to change something.

Red Pill: *The road between dreaming of being a master and the reality of being a master is long and paved with disciple, tenacity, intensity, and persistence. And there are no short-cuts.*

Therefore, if you want to be a master, you've got to love what you do. There is no human on earth who can endure the time and effort required to attain mastery unless they truly, deeply love the journey. So do what you really, really love—stuff that fulfils you and gives you joy enough to sustain you and keep you coming back for more.

Good enough is (generally) good enough

This mastery stuff is fine if you want to become a concert violinist or the next Elon Musk or a chess grandmaster, but for many (most) of us, the prospect of devoting 10,000 hours to just one thing is daunting, if not downright impossible. Many of us don't have the option to devote a decade to *just one thing*. In fact, most professions today demand such a broad variety of skills that spending 10,000 hours developing just one would be worthless.

It may take 10,000 hours to develop mastery, but the truth is that in many fields we really don't need mastery. *We don't need to achieve world champion status; we need "top 5%" status. We need* **competence**.

Luckily competence only takes a fraction of those 10,000 hours to attain. This is the rationale behind a new rule of thumb I encountered recently: the **100-hour Rule**.

The 10,000 hour rule is based on becoming the best of the best and as we have seen, that requires a tremendous amount of practice (and time and talent and opportunity and intensity and life changes) to reach the very top in a given field. But, the 100-hour Rule says,

It only takes 100 hours (give or take, depending on the discipline) to go from beginner to being better than 95% of the population—enough to make you competent, even to set you apart.

Now we're talking! 100 hours is doable! At 1 hour a day, you could become competent at a new skill in just over three months. If you put in some intense effort for just 20 minutes a day, you could become better than 95% of the population inside of one year! Think of that. So, pick a discipline: playing the guitar, karate, cooking, photography, running, whatever. 20 minutes a day of deep, intense practice or study (maybe with some coaching) and you'd be better than 95% of the entire population in that discipline.

That doesn't mean you're going to be the *best* guitar player or photographer but you'll be better than 95% of the population. The secret is *consistency*. It's the *compounding effect* of intense practice and study. And you can do it.

It still takes work, and it still requires deep practice: the active, deliberate, slightly uncomfortable kind that pushes you past your limits. It isn't a walk in the park, but you can do it.

You won't be a world master at this thing. But you'll be better than 95% of the population. And that is quite probably good enough.

I find that hugely encouraging. I hope you do too.

#10000hourrule
#100hourrule

19

PROFESSIONAL HELP HELPS

When I was about thirty, I started a business with an accountant friend of mine, Craig (the same guy who taught me to make a life-plan). Craig was an incredible guy with some deep wisdom. He'd grown up in an average middle-class home where unfortunately his father had been an alcoholic. As a result, the family's circumstances had slowly declined and so when his dad eventually died (relatively young) his mom was left with very little. So, she got a job as an agent selling houses and apartments. And she had to continue doing so until she was well past retirement age. One day Craig told me about the death of his mother:

Apparently, one Saturday afternoon she was preparing to show an apartment to a prospective buyer. She had unlocked the door and was waiting for the buyer to arrive when a drugged-up hoodlum burst in and stabbed Craig's elderly mom to death, for her cell phone. You can imagine the shock and anger and hurt and devastation that Craig and his family went through. But to his great credit, Craig took himself and his wife and his two small boys off to professional trauma counselling.

Craig told me that after two or three sessions, the counsellor had warned him and his wife to expect that one day, one or both of their little boys would act out the tragedy at home. But that they shouldn't be surprised, that this was part of the healing process and that they should allow it to happen and use it as a segway into a gentle and caring discussion where emotions and fears could be soothed and not stamped down. Well sure enough, that is exactly what happened: one day Craig walked into his elder son's bedroom and there he was stabbing his teddy with a pair of scissors. Craig was clear, if he hadn't been forewarned, he would likely have freaked and told the boy to stop it and been very hurt and angry and anxious for the kids' state of mind.

The fact that he had been forewarned however, meant that Craig was not freaked out, his response was pre-prepared, and it consisted of love and care and reassurance. Healing and closure were aided and not impeded.

> **Craigs' learning was this:** Every family should have a family psychologist in the same way as they have a family doctor. Someone who knows you well, with whom you check in regularly, who walks the long road of life with you and your family and who gives you good, wise, professional counsel along the way—good advice I think.

I really do believe in getting good, solid help and advice from properly qualified professionals and experienced mentors to help me think through the myriad of the issues of life from finances to career to my state of mind. And I encourage you to do the same.

Anyway, funny sequel to the story: after we started our business, Craig came to me one day and said, "You know Errol, I think we should appoint a business psychologist—someone who can help us deal with stress, or conflict in meetings, or teach us how to negotiate—someone who can walk the road of business with us and who can give us good, wise, professional counsel along the way." Great idea" I said, "Craig, you find someone." And so he did. And she was excellent. The only trouble was, she was also an absolute stunner! After my first one-on-one meeting with her I went back to Craig and said, "Listen buddy, I can't do this. This is going to lead to trouble. I can't sit alone in a room with a gorgeous, intelligent woman like that and have long and deep personal conversations and imagine that it's all going to be fine. I just don't want to put myself into that sort of situation. I'm a man, and I know what men are. And I know how wolves are killed (see Story #1). He looked at me thoughtfully, and then nodded. And that was the last session either of us had with that particular psychologist.

I hope you see the moral in this story as well.

Get a Coach

Coaching is a powerful tool that can help you achieve you goals and reach your full potential. Whether you want to excel in sports, business, music or any other area of success, a coach can provide guidance, support, and accountability that can make a huge difference in your success.

One of the biggest reasons that successful people have coaches is that coaches can provide objective feedback and help you identify areas for improvement. Often, when we're working on something, we're so close to it that we can't see our own blind spots. A coach can step back and give you an outsider's perspective, helping you to identify and overcome obstacles that you might not have been aware of.

Coaches can also help you stay motivated and focused. When you're working towards a big goal, it can be easy to get overwhelmed or lose sight of why you started in the first place. A coach can help you stay on track and remind you of the bigger picture, keeping you motivated and driven to achieve your goals.

One of the most famous examples of the importance of coaching is Tiger Woods. Tiger Woods is arguably the greatest golfer the world has ever seen, and he's had a coach throughout his entire career. His coach, Hank Haney, has been instrumental in helping him to refine his technique, stay focused, and achieve his incredible level of success. Tiger is a way better golfer than Hank will ever be, but Hank sees things in Tigers action, or his mental state or his fitness that Tiger would simply be blind to. And that makes all the difference.

Another example of the importance of coaching can be seen in the world of tennis. Most of the best tennis players in the world have coaches, and these coaches have played a vital role in helping them to reach their full potential. From Novak Djokovic to Rafael Nadal, these players have all had coaches that have helped them to hone their skills, stay motivated, and achieve great success.

Coaching isn't just for athletes, it's also essential for business leaders. Many of the most successful business leaders in the world have coaches who help them to develop their leadership skills and achieve their business goals. A coach can help you to identify your strengths and weaknesses, set goals and develop strategies to achieve them, and stay on track to reach your desired outcome.

A business coach can play a crucial role in helping entrepreneurs and business leaders achieve their goals and reach their full potential. A business coach can provide a range of services, including helping leaders to identify their strengths and weaknesses, set goals, develop strategies, and stay accountable for achieving their desired outcome.

One of the key roles of a business coach is to provide objective feedback and help you identify areas for improvement. A coach can help you to see your business from a fresh perspective and identify blind spots that might be holding you back. For example, a coach might help you to identify that you are not delegating effectively, which is causing you to become overwhelmed and burnt-out. The coach can then work with you to develop a plan to delegate more effectively and improve your work-life balance.

A business coach can also help you to develop your leadership skills and build a strong team. A coach can help you to identify your leadership style, understand how to effectively communicate with your team and create a positive work culture. They can also help you to develop a leadership development plan for yourself and for your team members, with the goal of creating a more cohesive, productive and engaged team.

A great example of a successful leader who has used a business coach is Bill Gates, the co-founder of Microsoft. Bill Gates has credited his coach, Warren Buffett, with teaching him important lessons about business strategy, leadership, and decision-making. Buffett has been a mentor and advisor to Gates for many years and has played a critical role in helping him to build Microsoft into one of the most successful companies in the world.

Another example of a leader who has benefited from a business coach is Oprah Winfrey. Oprah has credited her coach, Tony Robbins, with helping her to overcome her fears and insecurities, develop her leadership skills and achieve great success in her career. Robbins has worked with Oprah for many years, helping her to set goals, develop strategies and achieve her desired outcome.

So, if you want to be really good at something, you should get yourself a coach. A coach can help you to identify your blind spots, stay motivated, and achieve your goals. Whether you're an athlete, a business leader, a musician or anyone else, a coach can help you to reach your full potential and achieve great success. **So, if you're serious about achieving your goals, don't hesitate to get yourself the best coach you can afford.**

Get a Mentor

Being mentored is slightly different to being coached. Where coaching is about pursuing quite narrow and specific goals, mentoring is more about life in its broader context. It's about quality of life, joy, peace, spirituality, being a better father, wife, friend. Being more rounded and mindful, being better in relationships, being courageous and self-less, letting go of hurts, being positive and generous. Perseverance. Building others up. It's often more about observation and emulation, and less about training. It's about seeing the good in what and how others are doing things and trying to do likewise.

The world is full of incredibly wise and sensible people. And it will serve you very well to seek out some of these folks who can dispense wisdom based on real world experience and principle and intellect. Or better yet, who live their lives based on these attributes and who you can emulate.

Of course no-one is perfect. So don't expect your mentor to be either. Cut them some slack, they're human too, they WILL fall in some areas and make mistakes from time to time. As will you. That doesn't negate the value of their experience or what you can learn from their lives. You must engage your own brain and sift what they say and what examples they set so that you can extract the pearls which apply to you.

If possible, seek out mentors whom you can interact with physically, in conversation, over coffee or a beer, whom you can walk partway of the road of life with. Maybe a parent, or a beloved uncle, or a teacher, or a pastor. And you can have more than one. And they can (should) change over time.

For me, several of the mentors that I've had over the years died before I was even born—guys like Solomon, or Ernest Shackleton. Others, I've had the privilege of reading in their own words, Victor Frankel, or observing from afar in real life, Nelson Mandela. Others have flashed before me just for a moment on screen, like the father who helped his injured son across the finish line at the Barcelona Olympics in 1992. There can surely be few more eloquent examples of grit and determination on the part of the son, and love and fatherhood on the part of his dad, than in those few seconds.

> ▶ **WATCH THIS …**
> *https://www.youtube.com/watch?v=t2G8KVzTwfw*
> The unforgettable story of Britain's 400m runner Derek Redmond, whose hamstring snapped during his event but was determined to finish the race at the Barcelona 1992 Olympic Games.

My own father was a great mentor. He was a quiet, gentle man who loved his family and loved his wife—maybe the two most important examples a man could ever live out for his children. He also loved God and showed me to respect all living things.

One of my current mentors is Ray Dalio. A global macro investor for more than 50 years, Ray Dalio started out as a golf caddy. Later he founded Bridgewater Associates, building it into the largest hedge fund in the world. Dalio is the author of the 2017 book *Principles: Life & Work*, about corporate management and investment philosophy. In it he distils many interesting principles that I've been pondering on over the last few months.

What makes his work even more interesting is that he includes principles and ideas gathered from a wide "community" of employees and colleagues and counterparts.

READ THIS …

Principles: Life & Work by Ray Dalio. In it Dalio shares the principles that he developed, refined, and used over the past forty years to create stellar results in both life and business—and which any person or organization can adopt to help achieve their goals. One of my favourites.

Now I don't agree with everything that Dalio says. Nor in fact with everything my mother says. But that's the point of being an adult— look, listen, learn, ask, extract whatever wisdom you can and make up your own mind.

Here are a few of Dalio's principles …

1. Kindness is more important than you think.
2. There is no substitute for hard work.
3. The only substitute for working smart is working smarter.
4. Not everyone is going to like you and that's okay.

5. Find friends who are loyal and generous.
6. Be a loyal and generous friend.
7. Hire slow and fire fast.
8. Eat home cooked meals whenever possible.
9. Work out regularly and make the most of the time spent doing so.
10. Laugh at yourself.
11. Re-invent your relationship with your parents once you become an adult.
12. Think in decades not years.
13. Forgive people, it's easier than holding grudges.
14. Do things that scare you and translate the fear into excitement.
15. Work toward levelling the playing field for others
16. Ideas are cheap, execution is valuable.
17. Drink more water than you want.
18. There's only one earth, treat it right.
19. Giving becomes generous when it is uncomfortable.
20. Read good books.
21. Find hobbies and practice them.
22. If you don't measure it, you can't improve it.
23. Make data-based decisions.
24. Maybes are usually procrastinated no's.
25. Don't neglect the value of sleep.

#LifeCoach
#Mentor

20

THE PURSUIT OF HAPPINESS

We've covered a lot of stuff in the last few chapters, some of it quite heavy and serious. Well done for lasting! I hope you've found some true value along the way. Are you ready to go a bit deeper?

A LETTER TO MY CHILDREN

I want to share with you an important lesson which I've learned in my own life, and from wise mentors, and from reading some of the greatest thinkers and writers of history. It's about the pursuit of happiness.

Thomas Jefferson (1743–1826) was a bloke with a massive intellect and incredible insight into life (and, like most of us, a few blind spots in his own life). He is best remembered as the person who wrote much of the US Declaration of Independence. It includes these immortal words:

We hold these truths to be self-evident, that all men are created equal, that they are endowed by their creator with certain unalienable rights, that among these are life, liberty and the pursuit of happiness.

Brilliant! Inspiring.

Unfortunately nowadays, the "pursuit of happiness" is often seen as the primary goal of life. Marketers bombard us with messages and images of what a "happy" life looks like: generally, it involves perfect spouses and perfect children, living enviable lifestyles without a care in the world. Certainly nothing that is troublesome or depressive or burdensome. They define happiness as being able to "do whatever you want, whenever you want". And you're encouraged to do everything you can to achieve it. I'm sure that some well-meaning person has even told you "You *deserve* to be happy". Oh really? Sorry, no. Red Pill time.

You see, the problem with the pursuit of this superficial type of happiness is that it is so flimsy and fragile and unreliable. When life's storms come along (and they will); and you can't "do whatever you want, whenever you want", then that type of happiness is swept away and replaced by frustration and regret and resentment and emptiness.

It's far better to pursue something that is deeper and longer lasting than mere happiness. Far better to pursue something that is *meaningful*.

Things that give your life meaning are much, much deeper and more substantial than things that just make you happy. If happiness comes along for you (and I pray it does) then count yourself very blessed indeed but know this: happiness is not a human right.

Meaning will sustain you through the storms of life long after happiness has checked out.

So how do you find meaning?

Friedrich Nietzsche (1844–1900) was a German philosopher who challenged the foundations of religion and traditional morality. He concluded that a meaningful life requires the pursuit of something greater than oneself. And I agree.

He wrote, "He who has a *why* to live can bear almost any *how*." In other words, when we have a sense of purpose and meaning which transcends our personal self-interests, we are likely to be able to handle the hard stuff of life even in the absence of happiness.

In the same vein, **Dostoevsky** (1821–1881), the great Russian writer and philosopher, also conclud*ed that the pursuit of mean*ing was more important than the pursuit of happiness.

"The mystery of human existence lies not in just staying alive, but in finding something to live for."

—FYODOR DOSTOEVSKY

Dostoevsky was part of a group of intellectuals who propagated ideas of freedom and socialism and revolution in Tzarist Russia. In 1849, he and other members of his circle were arrested. He spent eight months in prison until one day the prisoners were led to a nearby Square. There the death sentence was pronounced, last rites were offered, and several prisoners were led out to be shot. At the last possible moment, a messenger burst in with the information that they'd been reprieved. It was in fact a mock-execution that was part of the punishment. One of the prisoners went permanently insane on the spot.

Dostoevsky was then sentenced to a Siberian prison labour camp where he endured terrible physical and mental trauma. Yet, like Nietzsche, he concluded that true happiness comes not from your circumstances, but from a sense of meaning and purpose in your life. He later wrote: "There is only one thing that I dread: not to be worthy of my sufferings."

Viktor Frankl (1905–1997) was a renowned psychiatrist who survived years of suffering and horror in the Nazi concentration camps of the Second World War. He recalled, "The thought of suicide was entertained by nearly everyone, if only for a brief time. It was born of the hopelessness of the situation … Life in a concentration camp tore open the human soul and exposed its depths".

> **READ THIS**
>
> *Man's Search for Meaning* by Viktor Frankl. This seminal and bestselling book has been called "one of the great books of our time". This book will change you. It's a must read.

But he also wrote: "We who lived in concentration camps can remember the men who walked through the huts comforting others, giving away their last piece of bread. They may have been few in number, but they offer sufficient proof that everything can be taken away from a man but one thing: the last of the human freedoms—to choose one's attitude in any given set of circumstances, to choose one's own way."

And so Frankl concluded: *"Happiness cannot be pursued; it must ensue, and it only does so as the unintended side effect of one's dedication to a cause greater than oneself or as the by-product of giving of oneself to someone else."*

In other words, happiness is a by-product of a meaningful life, not the goal in itself. When we focus solely on the pursuit of happiness, we find ourselves chasing a feeling that disappears under pressure. On the other hand, when we focus on dedicating ourselves to something greater than ourselves and to loving others, we develop a sense of purpose and meaning that can sustain us even in very difficult times. We need to look outward, not inward.

So my dear children, I urge you to pursue meaning in your lives rather than happiness. For ultimately that is the road to happiness.

Love,
Dad

21

TO DAUGHTERS

There can be few greater joys than having a daughter. Daughters are your delight and your pride. They embody love and kindness and empathy and nurture and hope for a better tomorrow. If I could give my daughter three things, it would be the confidence to always know her self-worth, the courage to chase her dreams and the certainty that she is deeply and unconditionally loved.

But I also understand that for many young women early adulthood can be quite overwhelming. If you're in your twenties or thirties, you may well be going through one of the most intense times of your life—falling in love, getting your heart broken, studying, choosing a spouse (or deciding to be single), having children (or struggling to have children or deciding not to have children), worrying about your weight or your looks, and your career, and feeling guilty about the impact of your career on your family etc etc etc. Huge decisions. Big stuff happening. All at the same time. And I'm sure I don't know even the half of it.

Maybe you didn't have a dad who made you feel loved and protected (and who exasperated you with his dad jokes and un-asked-for advice). Maybe you don't have a dad at all. Whatever your personal experience, in addition to some of the thoughts elsewhere in this book, I'd like to offer some specific pointers for young women, as of a dad to a beloved daughter.

And boys, be smart, you should read this chapter too.

You have a unique and very powerful role

Women have an incredibly important role to play in their families and in society. Families with good wives and good mothers thrive. As do businesses and societies with good female role models and leaders. This world needs you to be all you were created to be.

I want to encourage you to be women of integrity and honour and grace—women who bring hope and encouragement and joy and creativity and strength and peace. Women who stand up for what is right and true and who encourage others to grow and to blossom. Women who respect themselves and others, who are gentle and kind and compassionate. Women of wisdom and self-control. And above all, women who are channels of love into the world.

Never forget or underestimate the unique power and responsibility that you have as a woman to influence others for good. I hope that you have the courage and character to use that power and to accept that responsibility. And to use it wisely and well.

Now, the next few sections contain some life stuff that is really important for you to think about. Seriously, a lot of your future happiness will depend on it. But somehow, very few people seem to speak about this stuff. I don't know why—maybe because some of it may seem unfashionable and some a bit un-PC. I'm sorry if you feel that way at first, hopefully by the end you'll be saying "why didn't anyone tell me this stuff before?!". Anyway, I hope you have the maturity to see the Red Pills for what they are. At least to think about them with an open mind. And then, read the following chapter as well—it was written for women as much as for men. Off we go …

Choosing a man

Not everyone is called to marriage but for those that are, falling in love is the most incredible, scary, wonderful, frustrating adventure imaginable.

——— 66 ———

"I will have poetry in my life. And adventure. And love. Love above all. No ... not the artful postures of love, not playful and poetical games of love for the amusement of an evening but love that ... overthrows life. Unbiddable, ungovernable—like a riot in the heart, and nothing to be done, come ruin or rapture."

—MARC NORMAN, SHAKESPEARE IN LOVE: A SCREENPLAY

Finding the right husband is probably the greatest blessing you will ever experience. But identifying and nabbing Mr Right is not always so clear or so easy. And getting it wrong can lead to serious heartache.

> **Remember:** You get to choose your husband. But your children won't get to choose their father. It's super important to choose a husband who will also be a good father.

So, what sort of bloke should you look for? Can I suggest that you ...

- Choose a gentle man. A kind man: A great indicator is how he treats those weaker or much younger or much older than himself, those who can add no real value to him. Does he take the time and energy to add value to them? Is he kind and gentle with children? And patient and respectful with the elderly?
- Choose a man who takes commitment seriously, even when the going is tough.
- Choose a man who believes that there is something greater than himself. A higher power. With a higher moral law, who should be taken seriously and respected. More of this in Chapter 23.
- Watch out for men who aren't serious about you, or themselves, or their careers or their responsibilities. Who aren't ambitious. Men who can't name anything they would fight for—especially if it's not you.

- Avoid the lazy, self-absorbed, critical, excuse makers.
- Avoid the financially illiterate.
- Watch out for men who party too hard or too often. Or who are hooked on computer games or surfing the web late at night. Dragons lurk there. You know this.
- Beware of men with difficult personal histories—where there is substance abuse in their pasts, or infidelity, or violence. Those behaviours are often deeply ingrained and are quite likely to resurface later.
- Beware of men whose fathers were bad role models—violent or abusive or crass or crude. It takes extraordinary courage and character (and probably a spiritual awakening) to break from a difficult childhood. Of course it can be done, but more commonly adults will eventually mimic what has been modelled for them during their childhoods, both good and bad. Have your radar up on this one.
- Avoid men with any sort of mental health disorder—bipolar disorder, clinical depression, or sociopathy. You are NOT there to "fix" him. You can't.[13]
- Remember the red flags from chapter 7—if he's selfish, if he tries to control you, if he's the jealous type, or the angry type, or a gambler.

Sorry to sound so very serious here, I'm only trying to remind you of stuff you really, really need to think about. Take the Red Pills, for your own sake and for the sake of your children.

And now, how about some Green Flags? Here are a few things that suggest your squeeze might be a keeper:

- He "bigs-you-up" and affirms you to others when you're present, and when you're not,

---

13 To be clear, by "mental disorder", I'm referring to conditions which are characterized by a clinically significant disturbance in his cognition, emotional regulation, or behaviour. Not the usual mood fluctuations or short-lived emotional responses to the challenges of everyday life.

- He's a well-balanced, mature adult and he doesn't need you to make him happy. He's already happy within himself, you're just the cherry on top,
- He never and I mean ever flirts with anyone other than you. Not even casually,
- He's completely at ease leaving his unlocked and unattended phone in your possession. Not because you've told him to, but because he feels comfortable doing so (and you feel the same).

And remember; …

There is no "perfect". There will always be struggle. You just have to choose who you want to struggle with. Choose wisely.

Righto, moving on.

Let's say you're the type that does want to get married—you've found Mr Right. You've had your dream wedding and now you're "adulting"; here's a little insider information about your man—stuff to know for *your own benefit*:

What a man wants

It's generally quite simple really, most of us men want just three things: good food, good sex and good company. Not necessarily in that order and not necessarily even all three in the same time frame. Any two will do. At least for a while. But then you should rotate the third one into the mix, even if it means you rotate another one out. Try to keep the three nicely in balance over time. Of course, you'd be the perfect wife if you can keep all three going simultaneously all the time. But all three going simultaneously *some* of the time is good enough.

And here's the cool thing about good food, good sex and good company—they all benefit from *both* of you being involved. Cooking good food *together* can be a great space for good company to thrive. And good company easily leads to good sex, and so on. So be encouraged to do stuff together, like cooking, not as a sharing of the chore but as an opportunity for good company.

About nookie

Nookie deserves its own special mention. Love and sex are undeniably connected. But they are not the same thing. It's possible to have sex without being in love. Yet making "love" *without the love* seems rather empty I reckon—kind of settling for something lesser and cheaper.

On the other hand, if you are in a long-term committed romantic relationship, eventually, sex comes into play. One without the other is very unlikely to work for anyone in the long-term.

So let me say this straight off: I believe that sex is not only a wonderfully intimate physical act but it's also a deeply psychological and spiritual act of love. As such it should be valued and cherished and protected and reserved only for deeply committed relationships of love viz marriage.

Now most people would probably agree that men and woman see sex somewhat differently. Which can be very frustrating. The conventional perception is that women generally prioritise connectedness and emotion while men are more focused on the physical side. The implication of this perception is that therefore women are typically the somewhat resigned "givers" and that men are the somewhat selfish "takers" when it comes to sex. This is a monumentally damaging misrepresentation of a loving relationship. It is simply wrong to assume that men don't see sex as an extremely important component of emotional connectedness. Speaking as a man who has been married to the same wife for over thirty years, sex is the primary way a man bonds emotionally with his wife. Sex is the language men use to express their tender, loving, vulnerable feelings. It is their language of intimacy.

> The more important consideration therefore is not how society says we are different but how, in greater measure, men and women are the same.

Most people, irrespective of how they see sex, would agree that it is a humongously important part of a loving and healthy marriage relationship. There is a mountain of good wisdom written on this subject, plus several mountains of pure drivel, so be discerning with what you read.

READ THIS ...

https://www.betterhelp.com/advice/love/7-reasons-why-love-and-sex-go-together Betterhelp.com is a really good online resource covering many topics. Check it out.

The Five Love Languages by Gary Chapman. Chapman identifies five basic "languages" of love and that all of us speak. He then helps couples learn to speak and understand their own, and their partners love language, and to effectively love and feel loved in return. It's a great book, and a real aha read for most men. It was for me!

I thought I'd maybe just add a few realities on why sex is so important to your husband and, more importantly, *how that benefits YOU*:

1. Sex strengthens the relationship

Loving sex plays a vital role in emotional bonding. This is particularly true for men. We see sex as a way to solidify the relationship. When our wives happily and positively engage in nookie (i.e. not as a duty or a favour), they are actually telling us that we are their priority. Sex reassures us that we are united even at times when we might feel a bit distant. It is not only about physical contact, but also about reassuring each other that whatever else is happening, we're still together, exclusively, intimately as a couple.

2. Sex is way more effective than words

This may be the crucial difference between men and women. Most women are happy to agree that they are typically more emotional than most men. They react to kind words and gestures and for them expressing love through words and acts of kindness is an essential way of building intimacy.

In the same way, for married men, loving sex is worth a thousand of those words.

That doesn't mean we don't appreciate a loving gesture or kind words, but it does mean that there is nothing better a wife can do to express love than to happily enjoy some nookie. And if she initiates it, well that's just next level!

3. A lack of sex affects our confidence

Society expects men to be emotionally impregnable, but the truth is that we are every bit as vulnerable as you are. We're just socially conditioned to hide it, so we go quiet and withdraw. Or we get grumpy.

Society has conditioned us to believe that men should initiate sex, not women. Also, that men should be experts at sex and be able to *intuitively* know (because nice girls don't talk about sex) what you want, how and for how long. In short, the pressure to perform is immense on men.

So, imagine this scenario: Your husband puts himself out there—he sends you all the signals that he's up for some nookie. But you're not so keen, so you send some signals back—you ignore him, or you take evasive action: "I've got a headache", "the kids are awake", "I'm too tired", "I've got some work to do". You shut him down. And okay, he back's off. But believe me, he's feeling a bit stung. What he hears is: "I don't want sex with *you*", or "you're not very good at it, so why bother" or "I've got better / more important things to do".

How many times do you reckon you can shut him down like that before there's a problem? He goes quiet and resents. Or he gets grumpy. Or he goes elsewhere, maybe to a screen. Five times? Twice in a row? Three times?

Believe me, sex with their true love—the woman they would die for, is one of the things that keeps men going. Without it we lose confidence in our most intimate relationship, and in ourselves. It is a wrong perception that all men are selfish—good men want their wives to enjoy sex too and many are ready to go to great lengths to provide them that enjoyment. But we are not made of stone, if we keep getting shut down, we won't beg, we will simply opt out (at least emotionally). There is nothing better for a man's ego than when his wife sends the message that she *wants* to make love to him. When she sends that signal, believe me he can walk on water, do anything, achieve anything because what he hears is: "I believe in YOU, I love YOU, I want US".

> **In short:** Good, loving sex is very important for men AND for a healthy, loving marriage relationship. And therefore, it's very important for YOUR happiness as well.

So girls, make sure you give your husband plenty of "sugar". It's a gift that costs you nothing but is of immense value to him. Even if you don't feel like the full movie, the surprise short clip will be an investment in your relationship that will pay you brilliant dividends. Believe it. Apply the Nike slogan. ☺

And by the way, so long as it's a part of a full and healthy sex life, there's nothing wrong with rewarding your husband for something special he has done with a bit of thank-you-nookie. It shows him you've seen and appreciated the effort / thought / time / money / love he has put into doing something special for you. Be assured he's much more likely to do it again if you show him how much you appreciate it! And that's surely better than him feeling resentful that his efforts weren't noticed or appreciated.

One time a friend of mine, who didn't really like ballet, decided to surprise his wife with two tickets to see Swan Lake. She loved it and he endured it in good humour. When they got home, they pulled into the garage, and he was about to get out of the car when his wife said, "Just a moment darling ..." And she gave him a treat to remember. Believe me, he's much keener on ballet now! And so everyone's happy. Get it?

Now, if you're a woman reading this and it all comes across as a bit one-sided or maybe even a bit transactional, wait, you haven't read the next chapter yet ... I'm sure you'll be pleasantly surprised.

Stay with me ...

What a man needs (the other thing)

Your respect. Never ever, ever belittle your man, for example, by making fun of him in front of others (or even in private) or by dismissing his ideas, thoughts, and desires as stupid or silly.

Hollywood seems to think this is somehow funny. Popular culture propagates the narrative that men are not worthy of respect: they are all chauvinists, stupid, lazy, irresponsible, uncommitted, and shallow. Men abandon their families. Men cheat. Men are selfish. Men are violent. Men are losers. And therefore, they should be disrespected and laughed at.

Of course, it is certainly true that there are men who are some of these things. *These things do not, however, characterise men.*

Real men live by a very deep-seated honour code. They resonate with the idea of laying down their lives for those they love—you, the kids. Or for a cause that is bigger than themselves. There are many, many examples of this, especially in situations of great distress or war.

One of the most famous examples of this honour code is the true story of Lawrence Oates, an English polar explorer:

I'm just going outside.

In 1911 a British team led by Captain Robert Scott attempted to be the first humans to reach the South Pole, walking 895-miles (1,440 km) through the snow and ice, dragging their food behind them on wooden sleds. After persevering through tremendous hardships in viciously cold weather they reached the Pole on 17 January 1912 only to discover that the Norwegian explorer Roald Amundsen had beaten them to it. Gutted and demoralized the five-man team began the bitter hike back to their base. They never made it.

Hampered by worsening weather, poor provisioning, injury and frostbite, the team struggled on in ever-more desperate conditions. Edgar Evans was the first to die, as the result of a blow to his head when falling into a crevasse.

The four remaining men struggled on, slowed by fierce blizzard conditions. Captain Oates, severely frostbitten, with gangrenous feet and general weakness began to hold them back further so that they could not keep up the daily distances needed to reach provisions before their rations were exhausted. On 15 March Oates told the others that he could not continue, suggesting that they leave him in his sleeping-bag and go on without him. They refused.

The following night, according to Scott's diary entry, Oates said to his colleagues: "I am just going outside and may be some time." Then, he stepped outside into a raging blizzard and bitter temperatures to face certain death.

Oates sacrificed himself in an effort to save his comrades. Sadly, it was in vain because Scott, Wilson and Bowers died nine days later, eleven miles short of their next pre-laid food depot which might have saved their lives.

Oates' courage and self-sacrifice is the stuff that resonates in the heart of every honourable man. He longs to be needed, to be valued, to be worthy of the love and respect of his friends and family.

Disrespect tells a man that he isn't valued and isn't wanted. He starts to believe that he has become an object of resentment or ridicule, a burden, and that it might be better for everyone if he were just not there. So, he withdraws, he shrinks, he stops trying, he *becomes* what the disrespect tells him he is—diminished, a loser.

Or he leaves.

Your man needs to feel valued like you need to breathe. And know this: yours is the most important opinion in his life. More important than his boss's, more important than his friends, his colleagues, his parents. Your voice can shape him and determine who he can become. He may act tough, and confident and brash but deep down, as the poet and philosopher Henry David Thoreau wrote, "*Most men lead lives of quiet desperation.*"

In the quiet, when they're alone, most men will ask themselves, 'Am I good enough? Do I have what it takes to lead this family, to be a good father and husband and provider? Can I keep them safe and give them security and a future? Am I worthy of their respect?"

Wives, your man needs you to speak life into him. Your voice, your opinion matters. Much more than you realise. That is your power. So give him value, show him respect and I promise you, unless you have ignored every red flag in choosing him, he will live up to it. He will grow in stature and make you proud.

What a man needs (one more thing)

Men need adventure. And you will be doing him (and your family) a great service if you encourage him to seek it in the right places:

Men: Wired for Adventure[14]

I believe the desire for adventure is wired into the heart of every man. Now, not every man wants to go jump off cliffs or hang glide or hunt alligators in the Amazon. That's not what I mean by adventure. But every man needs a sense of risk in his life. Guys who e-trade stocks? That's adventure. Guys who are on the cutting edge of research science? That's adventure. These men are looking for discovery; they're looking for breakthrough.

That longing for adventure goes back to the time when guys were little boys. What do little boys love to do? They love to explore, they love to overcome challenges, and they want to simply go! Boys don't just want to ride their bikes. They want to ride their bikes with no hands! They want to jump them off the curb. They want to see who can go fastest down the hill. There really is something in every man that was wired for adventure from boyhood.

I think that sense of adventure gets tamed out of us. We also get frightened. Somewhere along the way, a man loses that confidence, that recklessness or fearlessness he had as a boy. Somewhere along the story of his life, doubt comes in. And a doubt goes like this: "No you don't. You don't have what it takes. You can't come through. You can't pull this off. So just put your nose to the horse in front of you and get in line and just become a gelding. Tie your reins up there at the corporate corral and give up any sense of risk."

I remember waking up one morning to realize that I hated my

---

14   By John Eldredge and Mark Elfstrand: https://www.cbn.com/entertainment/
books/menpassions-adventure.aspx?mobile=false&u=1

life. I'm wearing a suit and tie and I'm working in politics. And I don't like suits and ties and I don't like politics. I realized that somewhere along the way I had abandoned my dreams and my desires as a man.

To be a true man doesn't mean you have to go jump out of an airplane. To be a true man, you must live with courage and you must accept the risks that God is asking you to walk into.

Such risks may express themselves in lots of different ways, depending on the way a particular man is wired. For one man, the biggest risk in his life is writing that book he always wanted to write. For another man, it is taking a promotion which will put him into a leadership position that he doesn't know he can fulfil. For another man, the biggest risk of his life is actually selling his business and spending more time with his kids. The point is … courage.

I can certainly relate to this. I'm not one for extreme sports or crazy physical danger but give me a road trip on a lonely gravel road where I can explore for hundreds of miles, or a hike in the mountains—pure bliss. I feel free and invigorated and recharged. Something deep in my DNA says yes, I was born for this. I can breathe again.

Men need adventure. When men lack good adventures with good risks, they get bored and they get frustrated. And they become vulnerable to bad adventures with bad risks—they cheat, they drink too much, they spend too much, they drive recklessly, they gamble. And so on. You get the picture.

So girls, respectfully encourage your man to be everything he was created to be—more tomorrow than he was yesterday, to experience more, learn more, push his boundaries, explore, grow, bond with good male friends. Go fishing or exploring or riding or hiking. Encourage him to have some adventure in his life. He will bless you for it. And you will have exercised your influence for great good. His *and* yours.

And the same is true if you're a mom of boys. Boys need adventure too. That's why sport is so good for them. Try to limit saying: "be careful, come back here, climb down from there, slow down", too much. He needs a bit of danger in his life. It's in his DNA. Boys gain incredible things when they do dangerous things carefully. A few scrapes and bruises are a very worthwhile trade for a boy developing self-confidence and assurance.

READ THIS ...

Wild at Heart Expanded Edition: Discovering the Secret of a Man's Soul by John Eldredge. Somehow, somewhere between childhood and the struggles of the daily grind, most men lose sight of their dreams. God made men to embrace a life of courage, adventure and freedom, to take risks and find true purpose and belonging. This book invites men to recover their true heart. It's also a great read for women who wish to understand their men better.

As the woman you have 100% responsibility ...

- To make your house into a home, where everyone feels safe and loved and secure.
- To set the tone of the home. You need to model respect for everyone—from your husband to your children. You're allowed to get righteously angry but you should NEVER become verbally abusive. Don't provoke your husband or your children. Never belittle anyone.
- Your role is to nurture, to encourage, to build up—you're the coach and the cheerleader for everyone, husband as well as children.
- Stop worrying about things that aren't worth worrying about.
- Don't excessively sacrifice yourself for everyone else.
- Don't get too hung up about what other people think, especially on social media. In fact, don't worry too much about what other

people are thinking about you at all—they're not. And if they are, they're probably just wondering what *you're* thinking about them!

- Don't compare yourself too critically with other people, especially with what you see of them on social media—that's their glossy side, not their full self. Instead, be confident and content with your well-considered life choices.
- Look after yourself. Exercise. Read good stuff. Expand your mind. And rest. Read that last bit again. You have a responsibility to rest. It's super important. You can't do all this stuff if you're running on empty. Remember the chapter on juggling balls? Slow down. Simplify.

And by the way, you don't need to feel guilty about everything that goes wrong in life.

In God's economy you get points for effort and good intentions, not just outcomes.

Read that again. Believe it. Forgive yourself.

Good stuff ladies. Now read the next chapter. It's for you too.

#livewithpositiveintent
#findakindman
#rest
#simplify

22

TO SONS

I t's hard to put into words the joy of having honourable sons. Sons are your strong right arm. Your pride. They bring out the fun in you. They remind you of the sheer joy of mud and speed and laughter and silliness. They carry in them a sense of the future and of hope and progress and adventure.

Transitioning from boyhood to manhood is an incredibly important rite of passage. It is a time when a young man learns to take on more responsibility, both for himself and for those he cares about, and becomes more independent and self-sustaining. It's an exhilarating time as you begin to spread your wings and decide for yourself the type of person you want to be. But it can also be a daunting time as the demands on you, and the expectations of you, grow exponentially. Especially once you're a husband or father.

Maybe you were lucky enough to have a fully involved father (or other male) who was a good role-model. But maybe you weren't.

I hope this section provides a few thoughts that resonate with you … and please, also read the previous chapter, it was written as much for you as for her. You'll be surprised at the overlap.

You have a unique and very powerful role

Men have an incredibly important role to play in their families and in society. Families with good husbands and good fathers thrive. As do societies with good male role models and leaders.

We hear a lot in the media about "the patriarchy" and "masculinity" which are both typically labelled as "toxic". I'm not going to engage in those debates, other than to encourage you not to allow yourself to be conditioned into thinking that men are merely a sub-class of society which must, regrettably, be tolerated. **Encouraging women to be all that they were created to be, and removing societal barriers to that, does not equate to men becoming less than what they were created to be.**

On the contrary. I want to encourage you to be fathers and husbands and men of integrity and honour—men who bring hope and encouragement and joy and discipline and safety and peace. Men who stand up for what is right and true and who encourage others to grow and to blossom. Men who love others. Above all, men who love.

Never forget or underestimate the unique power that you have as a man to influence others for good. Use that power widely and deliberately.

—————— **66** ——————

"You have enemies? Good. That means you've stood up for something in your life."

—WINSTON CHURCHILL

A wise mentor once suggested that I write letters to my children on significant occasions in their lives (like a special birthday, or when they finish school or university, or when they get married). She suggested that these letters should be filled with positive reinforcement that will be a source of inspiration and encouragement for them whenever they re-read the letters, long into the future. And long after I'm gone. What great advice! Thank you Aunty Kathy.

Here's the letter I wrote to my daughter when she was 10:

TO MY DEAREST AND MOST PRECIOUS HANNI

How wonderful it is for a dad to write a love letter to his daughter!

It seems like yesterday that I watched you being born—in our bed, at home. Do you know that you changed my world? From the day we found out we were expecting you, Mom and I have loved you and prayed for you constantly. Our house was filled with love for you long before we ever knew who you would be to us and since the day you were born you have filled our lives with joy and laughter.

I fell completely, head-over-heels in love with you the instant I met you.

Now, 10 wonderful years later, I cannot tell you how proud I am of the young lady you are, and how thrilled I am to know you and to be your dad.

I want to thank you for who you are. I want to tell you how much you mean to me and how much I love you.

I love your gentleness, your kindness and politeness. I really appreciate your thoughtfulness to those around you. I love your giggles and constant happiness. I'm so very proud of your honesty, even when it gets you into trouble. I appreciate your obedience to Mom and me. I love your singing. I love your love of dressing-up. I love your sense of fun and playfulness with your brothers. I love the way your nose wrinkles up when you laugh. I love rubbing your tummy. I love it when you climb onto my lap. I love your adventurous spirit and your courage. I love your concern for animals.

Now, what should a dad say to his little girl on her 10th birthday? These years have been a wonderful adventure. The next ten will be even more so. As God wills it, you will finish school, you will become a teenager and finish being a teenager, you will become a woman, you will begin to shoulder more and more responsibility for your own choices and decisions. You will experience great joy and, probably, a few tears.

When you meet that special boy, the boy who will be like the air that you breathe, like the music to your soul; make sure that he is gentle with your heart, and you be gentle with his. Treasure your body, and his.

Treasure your friends. Laugh, sing and dance like no one's watching. Notice sunsets and flowers and do cartwheels in the rain.

No doubt you will also experience hardship and sadness. Do not be afraid of these times, they will deepen your character and enrich the courage and compassion you already have. At these times, be assured that no matter what, no matter how lonely or anxious or despondent you feel, God has a relentless, undying, unfathomable, unquenchable love from which you will never be separated. EVER! He will NEVER leave you nor forsake you. Whatever experiences the future holds for you, know that He will be experiencing them with you.

I pray that God will bless you mightily and fill you with His presence in a rich and powerful way.

I hope too that you will continue to allow me to be your friend. It will be a great privilege for me to share some of these things with you—the ups as well as the downs. I pray that I may be a worthy Dad and friend to you. Always.

My prayer for you today above all is that your life might be filled with love. May you have a deep and abiding sense of the love of your family. Thank you for filling our home with so much love and for being such a constant source of joy and pride.

And finally, Hanni, may you continue to love Jesus Christ with all your heart and mind and soul; and to be a channel of His love to this world.

I love you forever. God bless you, my precious little girl,

Dad

Men, choose to speak life and hope and virtue into your wife and children. Your words have massive power and mean the world to them. Much more than you can imagine.

Choosing a wife

As I said in the previous chapter, not everyone is called to marriage. For those who are, marrying the right person is the most wonderful thing imaginable. But if you fumble the ball on this one, your life can become a proper misery.

So, …

- Find a woman who believes that there is something greater than herself. A higher power. With a higher moral law, who is outside of time and space. Who should be taken seriously. More of this in Chapter 23.
- Find a woman who is gentle and caring and nurturing. And fun.
- Avoid women who are attention seeking or too self-centred (handy indicator: they're hooked on selfies), or too high-maintenance.
- Watch out for women who spend too much time on social media—it's addictive and likely to lead to their becoming dissatisfied with their lives and with what you can provide for the family.

- Avoid women who are financially reckless—the big spenders (especially of money that they didn't make), the socialites who are fixated on their image and the brands they wear.
- Beware the arch feminist who resents men.
- It's a Red Flag if she tries to constantly control you or change you.
- Beware the temper. Beware the bossy, shouty one.
- It's a Green Flag if she encourages you to be all you were created to be.
- Be willing to let go of some old friendships that are not conducive to married life.
- Nookie is there for both of you to be blessed. Do your best to bless her.
- You need her to respect you. Be worthy of her respect.

And here's the thing, as the head of the home you have a sacred duty and responsibility to establish a positive culture in your home …

As the man you have 100% responsibility

- Strive after insight and wisdom. Insight as to the true circumstances in any situation and then wisdom as to what to do about it. This is a biggie. It should be your mission in life.[15] Love your wife and your family more than you love yourself.
- Becoming a father is one thing. Being a father (and a husband) is something else. It's a commitment you should be prepared to sacrifice yourself for.
- You need to find ways to love your wife in ways that she knows it and feels it. You need to tell her. And show her. Often.
- And the same goes for your children. They need to know deep down in their guts that above all, even though you're not the

---

15   By "wisdom" I mean to have the skills to live life successfully. Start here: Read the Biblical Book of Proverbs, it's ancient and it's inspired. It'll blow you away.

perfect parent and they're not the perfect kids, when everything else is stripped away, that you truly, unconditionally love them—that when things go wrong, when they mess up badly, or when they're in a crisis, that you're the first person they come to. Not the last.

- The burden of leadership is yours—establish a leadership shadow that enables your family to thrive in security and stability and a deep-seated knowledge that no matter what, no matter how hard, YOU will be there. That you can be relied upon to do what is right and best for your family. That you have enough backbone to take difficult or unpopular decisions and to stand by them in the best interests of your family. And that you'll never stop trying. In short, you take absolute ownership, extreme ownership of everything that impacts the wellbeing of your family.

READ THIS ...

Extreme Ownership. How US Navy Seals Lead and Win by Jocko Willink and Leif Babin. This #1 bestseller describes many crucial leadership lessons distilled from the battlefield but equally applicable to many other facets of life. Essentially it comes down to taking *extreme, personal* ownership for ensuring good outcomes.

- No blaming.
- No complaining.
- No intimidating the wife or the kids. Ever.
- No abdicating of the responsibility to instil loving discipline in the kids.
- The burden of supporting the family is yours. It doesn't matter whether she earns more than you—that's great. But the responsibility remains yours.
- YOU set the tone of the home by your example—is it a respectful, encouraging, loving tone? Or a critical, selfish, disrespectful, angry tone?

One of my sons was kind enough to read a draft of this book and he reminded me that I'd left out something that is very important—**Be man enough to apologise to your kids**. He told me this was one of his stand-out memories as a child—that I had apologised to him when I'd behaved badly, gotten too angry or whatever, I can't even remember. But my apologising to him had sent him a message that I took ownership of my own behaviour, and that I loved him and respected him and that I wanted our relationship to be real and honest and positive and not to be based on power or on hypocrisy. Wow, just by saying "I'm really sorry my boy. Please forgive me".

- Stop worrying about things that aren't worth worrying about, or that you have no control over.
- It's way better to ACT to mitigate a problem than to worry about it without doing anything.
- And when the going gets tough and the wheels are in danger of coming off, it's YOUR responsibility to notice, and to get help:

Take the lead in getting help

I love my wife with all my heart. She is indeed "flesh of my flesh and bone of my bone". And she loves me just the same. I truly know that. But that's not to say that things are always plain sailing. We're both humans and subject to all the foibles that go with the common human condition. I have her permission to relate this story:

I can remember one time many years ago when, for what felt like a long time, we could barely stand one another! We bickered and shouted and blamed and argued and seethed and ignored and sulked. Eventually one evening we got into such a rage that she actually said to me "well if you hate it so much, why don't you just leave!". And I responded," this is MY house, YOU leave!". Imagine that! I hope you never ever get so angry that you say those words to your spouse. I'm ashamed even remembering it.

Anyway, neither of us did leave but in the stillness after that bomb burst something clicked in my brain and I knew that I had to do something to try to save the marriage. I was the head of the home, and therefore it was my responsibility to lead us out of the war zone. I also knew that I couldn't do it alone. I was too angry. And she was too angry. We needed an independent third party.

I didn't want to go to anyone who knew us or who was even in our community. And I wanted a qualified professional who was also a Christian.[16] Eventually I found a woman psychologist who was on the counselling staff at a church on the other side of town. So I made an appointment. I didn't consult the wife about this or discuss a convenient time, I just made the appointment and informed her. In my seething heart I secretly hoped she wouldn't turn-up, then I could blame her for not coming and for not caring enough about our marriage. I was in a bad, bad place.

Well, she did turn-up and we stomped into the counselling room staring straight ahead and keeping our social distance as if one of us had Covid. The woman who saw us was older than us, also married and also had children.[17] She made us sit next to one another other on a two-seat sofa (grrr).

---

16 I think these are two important considerations when choosing a councillor – (a) find a professional (someone who is formally trained and accountable to a professional body), and (b) someone who shares your worldview, who is likely to "get" where you're coming from.

17 This is the third important consideration: find someone with some real-life, personal experience relevant to what you're going through. A professional qualification with no life experience is not good enough.

And then she started to slowly and tactfully draw us out.

Long story short, after several sessions and tears and grinding of teeth and discussions that covered the pressures of our lives and careers and intimacy and children and our expectations and our anger, this woman drew things to an incredible, very practical conclusion:

She turned to me and said, "Errol, you're a strong personality. You can be quite intimidating. **You need to watch the tone with which you say things to your wife**. When you're too intense, or too direct or too confrontational, she can't hear whatever truth there may be in what you're saying. All she hears is your intensity. And so she responds, not with rational discussion, but with emotion. Or she jumps to a different topic as an escape mechanism. And that just makes you even more angry, but YOU'RE the cause. You need to watch your tonality so that she doesn't feel attacked. So that you can dialogue."

Then she turned to my wife: "Megan" she said, "**You need to listen to what he's actually saying, and not what you imagine he's saying**. Don't hear what he says and then multiply it by ten. If he's moaning about something then believe him that he's irritated about that one thing. He's not saying that he's also irritated about these other five things. He's talking about this one thing and he's only "so" irritated, not "SO" irritated. So keep the discussion confined to its own, correctly sized box. Do not put other discussion topics in the box until you've resolved the topic already in the box. And don't inflate the topic so that it becomes bigger than the box for which it was intended."

We both took these insights to heart and, although we both still get it wrong from time to time, that counsellor's wisdom (and God's grace) saved our marriage. Of that I have no doubt.

The point I'm coming to is this: Men, as the head of your home, it's on you to have your radar up for situations, circumstances and attitudes that might endanger your family and the relationships in it. Be vigilant. Be on the lookout for incoming missiles or hidden landmines. And act. Real men don't bury their heads in the sand. They examine themselves. They're not in denial. When the car engine makes a strange noise, they take it to an expert to get it sorted. You should do the same when relationships in your family are misfiring. It's your job. That's what leadership in the home is all about. Taking Ownership.

> **Remember:** Asking for help isn't giving up. It's refusing to give up. And that takes courage. Be a man of courage.

You Need Adventure

You're not designed to spend your entire life in front of a computer screen. Or in a small office cubicle (*aka the abattoir of the soul*). Get out there. Explore.

Here's a thing about life … you are not going to get to the end and wish you had travelled *less*.

Make sure you live. And don't let making a living choke *actual living* out of you. Go on adventures. Take your family on adventures. Be the catalyst for making memories and expanding your (and their) horizons.

All men die.
But not all men truly live.

—WILLIAM WALLACE

About Nookie

If you're a bloke, I bet you were wondering when I would get to this part! We spent quite a bit of time on nookie in the previous chapter. I made the point strongly that sex is very important to you, and therefore to your marriage, and therefore it's to her benefit as well. (You're welcome). Now, I'm going to say the same thing to you, but from the other perspective:

Sexual love is an important aspect of a fulfilling marriage for women as well as for men, no doubt about that. But it is not the only aspect.

You need to understand that to build a strong and loving relationship, you need to prioritize other aspects of the relationship, including emotional connection, communication, trust, and mutual respect. Not just physical intimacy. And it's on you. Sorry, don't expect "sugar" if you haven't created an atmosphere of love, respect, honesty, and emotional security.

Okay, so how to do that? Well, understand that *non-sexual affection* is one of the key ingredients that women want in a marriage relationship. This includes simple gestures like holding hands, hugging, or cuddling on the couch. These non-sexual forms of physical intimacy help her feel more connected and valued and provide a sense of comfort and security in the relationship.

Honour and respect are important for her (just as they are for you). This includes being treated as an *equal* partner in the relationship, with opinions and contributions that are valued and respected. It also includes being treated with kindness, compassion, and empathy, even during difficult times.

Feeling loved is a crucial component of a successful marriage for women. So you've got to *tell* her. With sincerity. Often. And you've got to *show* her through actions, such as working hard for the family, giving her little surprise gifts, kind words and simply being present and attentive in the relationship.

Ultimately, what women want in a marriage relationship can vary widely depending on her individual personality. ***But understand this****: you prioritizing non-sexual affection will very likely end up in a lot more nookie than if you don't. Weird world huh? But there you have it.*

RELATIONSHIP TIP:

Wait until she's drifting off to sleep, then lean over and whisper into her ear how much you love her, and treasure her and honour her, and thank God for her. Then put your arm around her and go to sleep. Repeat often.

#LeadingMeansLoving
#MaleRoleModel
#HealthyMasculinity

23

THERE'S SOMETHING BIGGER THAN YOU

I believe that all humans exist with some sense of the divine wired into their sub-conscious minds. The vast, vast, vast majority of everyone who has ever lived has somehow sensed that there is something greater than him- or herself. A higher power. With a higher moral law, who is outside of time and space. Who should be taken seriously.

Now I fully appreciate that there are some people who flatly deny this. They say there is no God, that faith is childish and foolish, and that science has disproved religion. They hold that everything we see around us in this world and beyond it is simply the result of completely random, completely spontaneous arrangements of atoms which, over billions and billions of years have combined and re-combined and finally agglomerated, purely by chance, into "life". And then these ancient life-forms slowly, through natural selection, evolved into ever higher forms of life which reproduced themselves by contributing very selected matter derived from themselves to other very similar but not-quite-the-same life forms in a way such that a new life would result. Not only that, but these primitive life forms could also sustain themselves by converting light or heat to energy or by ingesting and metabolising other, spontaneously occurring life-forms.

Okay if you believe all of that can arise spontaneously and randomly, then I must say I admire your faith. That's the type of faith that says:

if you leave a pile of ingredients, milk and eggs and salt and meat and whatnot on a table and every so often a tornado rips through your house and randomly re-arranges all the ingredients and randomly adds just the right amount of energy, then, sooner or later, you'd spontaneously end up with a hamburger. Seems like a bit of a reach, doesn't it?

I'm the sort of guy who considers it much more sensible and logical to assume that a hamburger results from the intentional actions of an actual chef rather than from a sequence of completely random and spontaneous events. In the same way I believe that it is much more feasible and logical to believe that there *is* an intelligent designer behind the incredibly intricate and beautiful and interconnected and immense universe we see all around us.

I simply don't have enough faith to believe that everything exists by pure chance as the result of millions of random and spontaneous events that somehow "stuck" and then progressed to ever more intricate and sophisticated levels. I reckon it's much more rational and logical to believe that there is a higher intelligent power. Who is outside of time and space. And who determines it all. Call him the Intelligent Designer, or the Original Chef, or the Great Spirit if you like. I call him "God".

That said, I do acknowledge that there often seems to be tremendous tension between people in the areas of faith and science. Many people feel pressured to choose between the two, as if it's an "either/or" situation. But that's simply not the case. Upon closer examination, it quickly becomes evident that faith and science are *not* mutually exclusive: one is focused on the nature of truth (scripture), and the other on the truth of nature (science). To insist that truth lies in only one or the other domain is only half the story, as in watching trees swaying and bending without recognizing the presence of the wind.[18] Scripture emphasizes

---

18   *God and Galileo* by David Block and Kenneth Freeman. 2019. Crossway.

our place in the universe as *spiritual beings* and the direction of God's plan for us and his relationship with us. Faith in God never requires that our reason, or scientific method or observation, must be jettisoned. Absolutely not. But these are not its purpose or focus.

Similarly, science is focused on what can be observed and measured or inferred by theoretical means. It has very little to say about *spirituality* or *meaning* or *beauty* or even *love*. Scripture does not address all that there is to know about space or quantum physics or ballistic missiles, but on the other hand, it is completely beyond the domain of science to conclude that mankind has no soul and no eternal purpose and no connection with any higher power simply because it hasn't (yet) found an equation to describe these things.

Properly and fully understood, there is no conflict between scripture and science. Both can be and *are* true. They're just looking at things from different perspectives. I think the realisation that your *perspective matters*, is a massive step forward in *how* to think about truths which might at first appear to be in conflict but which, with deeper understanding, are seen to be fully compatible! I hope you find that re-assuring.

Now, it's interesting that the Bible never tries to prove the existence of God, it takes his existence as self-evident and obvious. For the writers of scripture, it's not a question of "Do you believe in God?" which is a question on the same level as "Do you believe in the wind?"

Since for them the existence of God is self-evident and undeniable, their real question is *"Do you believe God?"*. That is, "Do you believe what He *says*?" I've decided that I do. And I believe that what he says is contained in the Bible, and so I reckon it's a good idea to read it.

I'm a Christian because I believe the Bible to be true and also I believe that Jesus was speaking the truth when he claimed to be God in person. I arrived at this belief after a lot of thought and study and questioning and consideration of many alternatives. The implications of this belief are by far the most important and far reaching of anything I will ever believe in my life, about anything.

Now relax, I'm not going to launch into an exhaustive defence of my belief that Jesus is God (you can check out the reading panel instead) but here's a simple line of reasoning which may resonate with you:[19]

Most educated people acknowledge that Jesus was a real historical figure and that he did actually exist—there is so much non-biblical historical evidence for this, that to deny it simply demonstrates ignorance or bloody mindedness. Sorry if that offends some people, but it's true.

On the other hand, while many people accept that he did exist, they say that Jesus "was just a good man"—a type of guru with well-intentioned, wise teachings. They can accept that he *existed*, but they don't believe he was *God*.

Okay, so let's test that logic: Either Jesus was who he claimed to be, or he intentionally lied and deceived many people (and was willing

---

19 Ron Reid. Growing Christian Ministries. 2022. https://www.growingchristians.org/devotions/more-than-a-good-man

to stand by his lies under the most gruesome torture and death sentence); or else he was mentally ill and delusional.

There are only five possible rational options:

1. Jesus is only a legend. A myth.
2. Jesus was a great moral leader. But that's all.
3. Jesus was insane.
4. Jesus was a liar. Or,
5. Jesus was, and is, who he says he is: God.

So, let's take a closer look at these five options, the logic is illustrated in the diagram below:

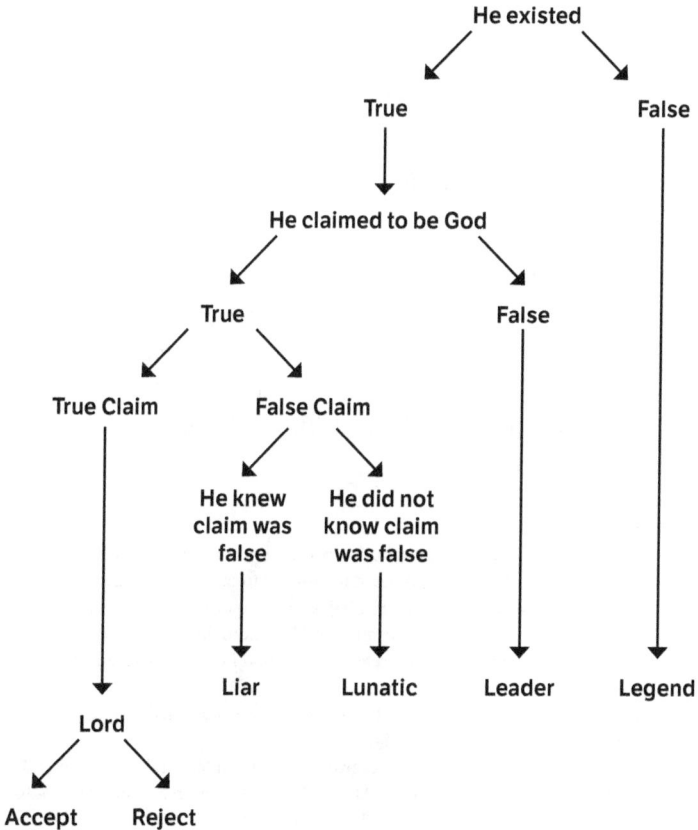

```
                        He existed
                       ↙          ↘
                   True            False
                     ↓                ↓
            He claimed to be God       ↓
               ↙          ↘            ↓
            True          False        ↓
          ↙      ↘          ↓          ↓
  True Claim   False Claim   ↓          ↓
      ↓         ↙      ↘     ↓          ↓
      ↓   He knew   He did not ↓        ↓
      ↓   claim was  know claim ↓       ↓
      ↓    false     was false  ↓       ↓
      ↓       ↓         ↓        ↓       ↓
      ↓     Liar     Lunatic   Leader  Legend
     Lord
   ↙      ↘
Accept   Reject
```

Just a legend?

Very few people believe that Jesus is only a legend. As I said, there's just too much historical evidence for His existence. Apart from eye-witness accounts in the Bible from people who actually knew him, some of the most trusted non-Christian writers of the 1st century (such as the historians Josephus[20] and Tacitus[21]) also mention Jesus. Throughout the ages, even opponents of Christianity never credibly doubted the historicity of Jesus. Even Muslims[22] and many Hindus accept that Jesus did exist, physically on this earth.

Consider also that many early Christ-followers (including all but one of His closest friends, his disciples) were brutally martyred for their belief in Him—burned alive, crucified and stoned. Would Jesus' disciples have been willing martyrs for a story they *knew* was a lie, or for someone who they knew never existed?

To believe that Jesus is just a legend is simply not a reasonable option. The historical evidence for His existence is simply too overwhelming.

Just a moral leader?

Acknowledging that Jesus is more than a legend is not difficult for most people. However, it's still not easy for many to accept that Jesus was and is God. Much easier to say He was just a good moral teacher and leader but only ever a human. This is the position that most non-Christians prefer to take.

---

20 There are two references in Josephus's writings that are commonly discussed in relation to Jesus. The most significant mention is found in Josephus's Antiquities of the Jews, specifically in Book 18, Chapter 3, Paragraph 3. This passage, commonly referred to as the Testimonium Flavianum, includes a description of Jesus and his impact. Another reference is found in Book 20, Chapter 9, Paragraph 1.

21 The Roman historian Tacitus mentions Jesus in his work called "Annals", specifically in Book 15, Chapter 44.

22 Some references from the Quran regarding Jesus include: Surah Al-Imran (3:47-49), Surah An-Nisa (4:171), Surah Al-Ma'idah (5:75), Surah Maryam (19:16-34), Surah Al-Ma'idah (5:110), and Surah Al-Anbiya (21:91).

The problem with this viewpoint is that the Bible says that Jesus did claim to be God. He made some radical statements about His deity. In fact, His claims to be God are often interwoven with His great moral and ethical teachings (which most people accept as good and noble sayings). It's unreasonable to attempt to separate these teachings.

There's no logical basis for accepting the "ethical sayings" of Jesus as historical, but then rejecting His claims to Deity as non-historical creations. The historical evidence overwhelmingly favours the position that Jesus claimed to be God. The position that Jesus was just a great human leader is not a logical option. Truly great human leaders don't make false claims about being God. Unless …

A Liar or Insane?

At this point a person must decide, "Was Jesus' claim to be God true, or was it a false claim?" If it was a true claim, then all of history past, present and future turns on this truth. If it was a false claim, then it was an outrageous lie.

But some people would say that Jesus wasn't deliberately lying. They would say He really did *think* He was God, but He was mistaken. If that was the case, then He was delusional, insane. If Jesus made the false claim that He was God, then He was either a liar or He was mentally ill. These are the only two logical options.

If Jesus was a liar, then He was a very unusual liar. Liars have a pattern of frequent lying—especially to protect themselves. They wouldn't stick to their false story if they were facing Roman crucifixion! Some people have bravely died for a lie, but at least they *thought* it was the truth. If Jesus was a liar, then He suffered through the most painful death for what He knew was a lie.

Habitual liars typically have other character flaws too. They don't have the consistency and dignity and authority that the historical records attribute to Jesus. Liars tend to be self-seeking, but Jesus was just the opposite—he cared for others to an extent and in ways that were remarkable. He just doesn't fit the mould of a liar in any logical way.

The same basic argument could be used for Jesus being delusional. Persons who are mentally ill typically exhibit abnormal personalities and unusual behaviour. Some mentally ill people think that they're God, or Napoleon, but they also display other unbalanced and even schizophrenic behaviour patterns. Jesus, on the other hand, was composed and in control of Himself. Massive crowds of people followed Jesus and listened in awe to His words. Little children were attracted to Him. Jesus' disposition and balanced personality were certainly not the traits of an unbalanced person. It's illogical to believe that Jesus was mentally unstable.

So what's left?

If logic excludes the legend, leader, liar or delusional ideas, there's only one option left. Jesus Christ proclaimed the truth when He claimed to be God. He *is* God.

Hmmm. Decision time?

Now I don't hang my faith on this logic alone dear friend, there is so much more which reinforces and informs my thinking and which gives me reason enough to be a Christian. For instance, the huge number of detailed prophesies about the future Christ which appear throughout scripture, and which were written hundreds of years before Jesus lived, but which he fully and *uniquely* fulfilled. I would urge you, above all else, to give serious and deep consideration to who YOU say Jesus was. It will transform your future for eternity.

If you need more, then read this …

READ THIS ...

The Case for Christ: A Journalist's Personal Investigation of the Evidence for Jesus by Lee Strobel. Is there credible evidence that Jesus really is the Son of God? Former atheist and investigative journalist Lee Strobel takes a look at the evidence from the fields of science, philosophy, and history. He cross-examines a dozen experts with doctorates from schools such as Cambridge, Princeton, and Brandeis, asking hard-hitting questions and arriving at a compelling conclusion. A comprehensive read for the true seeker.

Evidence for the Historical Jesus: Is the Jesus of History the Christ of Faith? by Gary R. Habermas. Habermas addresses the debate over the historical Jesus and shows a significant number of historical facts about Jesus in secular and non-New Testament sources that prove that the Jesus of history is the same Jesus of the Christian faith. Another great read if you have a mind for facts.

24

NOW WHAT?

I f you've gotten this far, then I must commend you. You're clearly serious about yourself and serious about your future. And about your impact in this world.

I'd like to just circle back to where we started: To quote Stephen Covey: *You are not a product of your circumstances. You are a product of your decisions.* So do whatever you can to make good decisions. As consistently as you can. But also important: don't over-sweat your failures. Learn from them and move on.

Also, remember that there was a time when you were a great winner. And, that *you* were deemed to be worthy of hope and a future. That's still who you are.

Simplify your life. Rest. Be kind. Forgive. Say no. Don't ignore Red Flags. Be serious about money and your career and your personal brand. Look after your health and your wellness. Love.

Strive to pursue meaning over happiness. For ultimately, that is the only road to true happiness.

If I could give you just three things, they would be the confidence to always know your self-worth, the courage to chase your dreams and the certainty that you are deeply and unconditionally loved by one who is greater than all of us—the living God who has had you in his mind since the beginning of time. He is for you. And always has been. And always will be.

———
"

"For what it's worth: it's never too late ... to be whoever you want to be. There's no time limit. Start whenever you want. You can change. Or stay the same. There are no rules to this thing. You can make the best or the worst of it. I hope you make the best of it. I hope you see things that startle you. I hope you feel things you never felt before. I hope you meet people with a different point of view. I hope you live a life you're proud of. And if you find that you're not, I hope you have the strength to start all over again."

—BENJAMIN BUTTON, THE CURIOUS CASE OF BENJAMIN BUTTON

25

TO MY FUTURE SELF

Well, enough of me nattering on to all of you! I guess it's about time I wrote some notes to myself for future reference. Kids take note—you're going to have to hold me to these:

So, assuming the wife and I are spared a few more years ...

- I will NOT be one of those blokes who resists moving into a retirement complex because that's for "old" people, or because I just can't bear the hassle and emotion of packing up and selling the family home. Instead, I will put my name down on the waiting list of several different complexes before I turn 60. Then I will sell up and move into my preferred retirement complex before I turn 70.
- I will NOT become a grumpy old codger who complains endlessly about the state of the nation, the new generation or the cost of living.
- I will endeavour to grow old with grace and dignity.
- I will ensure that I include young people in my regular social circle. And I will make a concerted effort to be interested in what they're interested in (even their music!), to engage them in conversation and to understand and learn from their perspectives.
- I will be interested and interesting. I will keep up with the news, and with sports and with culture and the state of the economy.
- I will use modern technology, especially that which enables me to keep in better contact with distant friends and family.
- My default response to every invitation to any social engagement or visit will be YES.

- I will endeavour to travel and by so doing broaden my mind and my knowledge of other cultures and their histories and their cuisine and their beer, wine, whiskey, and coffee.
- I will be politely sceptical about political, financial, medical and religious conspiracy theories that others pick up on social media.
- I will laugh a lot. And try to make others laugh too.
- I will memorise jokes and amusing stories and tell these whenever appropriate. And also sometimes when not appropriate.
- I will make a smile my default facial expression.
- I will resist the urge to tell everyone about my health and medical treatments.
- I will stop driving the car when my children kindly and lovingly suggest that it may be time to do so.
- I will watch girls walk by.
- I will wear my hearing aid. And mostly have it switched on.
- Regarding my adult children and grandchildren, I will keep my opinions to myself and the welcome mat out.
- I will be physically active for as long as I can and keep as fit as I can.
- I will use every opportunity to call or visit my children and grandchildren, at their convenience. When they invite me over or on a trip, my default answer will be YES.
- I will read good literature for entertainment and enlightenment. And listen to good music.
- I will dance.
- I will use a walking stick to mitigate the risk of falling when my children kindly and lovingly suggest that it may be time to do so.
- I will choose the humiliation of wearing adult diapers over the humiliation of wetting my bed and having someone else clean the sheets. Who knows, maybe I'll even grow so far in my self-acceptance that I won't view incontinence as humiliation.
- I'll smell nice so young people (such as nurses ☺) will sit by me and hold my hand.
- If I'm hurt or angered by what's happening to me or my body, I will do my best not to take it out on those who care for me.

- I will mind my personal grooming—I'll dress well, in clean clothes and get a regular haircut. I'll mind my personal cleanliness and hygiene.
- I will be kind. And respectful and polite. I will apologise.
- I won't pass wind in company, thinking no one will notice.
- And finally, when the time comes to finally shuffle off this mortal coil, my wife will dress in a black leather crop-top and leggings with tassels and high heels. We'll race my Harley off the edge of a cliff and she'll flick the pins out of the two hand grenades that she'll be holding, one in each hand. And we'll meet the Almighty with a loud bang in a burst of flame. (She hasn't fully bought into this plan just yet, but I'm working on it).

Seriously kids, if I'm ever too sick to make my own decisions, please let me go. Switch off the machines. Stop the meds. Sooner rather than later. I'd much rather you spent the money on a holiday having fun together and celebrating my life and looking after Mom than vaporising it on my medical bills. I know where I'm going, I'll see you there.

With deepest affection, love and blessings to you all,

Cheers,
Dad

ONLINE REFERENCES AND LINKS

For more in this line, and to buy this book (and all the others referenced below), visit **www.some-stuff.co**.

CHAPTER 1: JUMPING RIGHT IN
Read this: *To Own a Dragon: Reflections on Growing Up Without a Father* by Donald Miller and John MacMurray. This is an inspiring read for anyone who didn't grow up with a good father. And for everyone who want to be one.
CHAPTER 4: SOME BALLS BOUNCE
Watch this: *https://www.youtube.com/embed/UF8uR6Z6KLc* Apple founder, Steve Jobs', famous announcement speech at Stanford University.
Read this: *The 80/20 Principle: The Secret of Achieving More with Less* by Richard Koch. The 80/20 principle is one of the great secrets of highly effective people and organizations. Koch shows how you can achieve much more with much less effort, time, and resources, simply by identifying and focusing your efforts on the 20 percent that really counts. An essential read.
Read this: *Simplify: How the Best Businesses in the World Succeed* by Richard Koch, Greg Lockwood. This book takes the 80/20 Principle to the next level. It's rocket fuel for any business.
CHAPTER 5: YOU'RE TOUGHER THAN YOU THINK
Read this: *Living With a Seal* by Jesse Itzler. At turns hilarious and inspiring, *Living With a Seal* ultimately shows you the benefits of stepping out of your comfort zone.

CHAPTER 7: DON'T IGNORE RED FLAGS

Read this: *Emotional Intelligence: Why It Can Matter More Than IQ* by Daniel Goleman. EQ includes self-awareness and impulse control, persistence, zeal, and self-motivation, empathy and social deftness. Far more than IQ, these are the qualities that mark people who excel in life, whose relationships flourish, who are stars in the workplace.

Read this: *Emotional Intelligence 2.0* by Travis Bradberry and Jean Greaves. Knowing what EQ is and knowing how to use it to improve your life are two very different things. This book delivers a step-by-step program for increasing your EQ to enable you to achieve your fullest potential.

CHAPTER 12: WHAT YOU NEED TO KNOW ABOUT MONEY

Read this: *The Index Card: Why Personal Finance Doesn't Have to Be Complicated* by Harold Pollack and Helaine Olen. This is a truly freeing read for anyone who feels lost about their finances. Inside is an easy-to-follow action plan that works in good times and bad, giving you the tools, knowledge, and confidence to seize control of your financial life.

Listen to this: *https://freakonomics.com/podcast/everything-always-wanted-know-money-afraid-ask* Freakonomics Radio Podcast (episode 298). Everything you always wanted to know about money (but where too afraid to ask).

Listen to this: *https://freakonomics.com/podcast/stupid-est-money* Freakonomics Radio Podcast (episode 297). The stupidest thing you can do with your money.

Visit here: *https://create.microsoft.com/en-us/templates/budgets* Free Microsoft Excel templates to help you set up a budget.

CHAPTER 14: BUILD RAPPORT

Read this: *How to win friends and influence people* by Dale Carnegie. One of the best-selling books of all time, the rock-solid, time-tested advice in this book has carried thousands of people up the ladder of success in their business and personal lives. Do yourself a favour and read it.

Read this: *How to Talk to Anyone: 92 Little Communication Tricks for Big Success in Relationships* by Leil Lowndes. This is a great book to help you master the art of verbal communication in your personal life and in business. An easy read.

Read this: *Influence: The Psychology of Persuasion* by Robert B. Cialdini. This highly acclaimed bestseller explains the psychology of why people say yes and how to apply these principles ethically in business and everyday situations. You'll learn the six universal principles of influence and how to use them to become a skilled persuader—and, just as importantly, how to defend yourself against dishonest influence attempts.

Read this: *The new Articulate Executive: Look, Act and Sound Like a Leader* by Granville N. Toogood. The simple truth is this: You need to look, act, and sound like a leader to succeed in today's business world. Whether you are giving a speech, making a presentation, conducting a meeting, or simply talking one-on-one, these tried-and-true communication techniques are guaranteed to help you step up your game. and speak like a pro.

CHAPTER 16: ABOUT YOUR CAREER

Read this: *Courageous Leadership: Field-tested strategy for the 360° Leader* by Bill Hybels. This book is one of the best books on leadership I've ever read. It's crisp, simple and easy to read. Start with this one.

Read this: *Leadership Axioms* by Bill Hybels. Another great but easy read on Leadership with plenty of practical tips that you can start applying immediately.

CHAPTER 17: DOING YOUR OWN THING

Read this: *Good to Great: Why Some Companies Make the Leap... and Others Don't* by Jim Collins—A classic business book that examines why some companies succeed while others fail, and what makes the difference. The book provides practical insights for entrepreneurs looking to build great businesses.

Read this: *The Lean Entrepreneur: How Visionaries Create Products, Innovate with New Ventures, and Disrupt Markets* by Brant Cooper and Patrick Vlaskovits. This book provides a framework for entrepreneurs to build successful businesses by focusing on the most critical tasks, while ignoring the rest.

Read this: *The Laptop Millionaire: How Anyone Can Escape the 9 to 5 and Make Money Online* by Mark Anastasi. This book provides easy to follow step-by-step strategies you can use to make money online.

WEBLINKS IN CHAPTER 17 UNDER THE SECTION: THE LAPTOP LIFESTYLE

- **Types of side hustles:** *www.sidehustlestack.co* and *https://sidehusl.com*
- **Get paid to read and review books online:** *https://onlinebookclub.org*
- **Get paid to take online marketing surveys:** *www.surveyjunkie.com*
- **Online tutoring:** *https://tutorme.com* and *https://www.chegg.com/uversity*
- **Freelance:** *https://www.upwork.com* and *https://www.fiverr.com*
- **Selling products online:** Amazon *https://affiliate-program.amazon.com* and Etsy *https://www.etsy.com/affiliates*

WEBLINKS IN CHAPTER 17 UNDER THE SECTION: AFFILIATE PROGRAMS

- **Affiliate Networks:** These are platforms that connect merchants with affiliate marketers. Some popular affiliate networks include *Commission Junction*, *ClickBank*, and *Amazon Associates*.
- **Link Tracking and Management Tools:** These tools allow you to track clicks on your affiliate links, so you can see which links are performing well and which are not. Some popular link tracking tools include *LinkTrackr* and *ClickMeter*.
- **Analytics and Reporting Tools:** Some popular analytics and reporting tools include *Google Analytics* and *Google Search Console*.
- **Email Marketing Tools:** These tools allow you to send promotional emails to your audience, which can be a great way to drive sales. Some popular email marketing tools include *Mailchimp* and *Aweber*.

- **Social Media Management Tools:** These tools allow you to schedule and post content to your social media accounts, which can be a great way to promote your affiliate products. Some popular social media management tools include *Hootsuite* and *Buffer*.

- **Content Creation Tools:** Some popular content creation tools include *Canva*, *Adobe Premiere Pro* and *Audacity*.

CHAPTER 18: MASTERY OR COMPETENCE

Read this: *Mastery* by Robert Greene. Greene mines the biographies of great historical figures for the common ingredients required to become a "master" in any field. He demonstrates how humans are hardwired for achievement—it's a canny and erudite explanation of just what it takes to be great.

Read this: *Outliers* by Malcolm Gladwell. The brilliant and entertaining book investigates what sets high achievers apart—from Bill Gates to the Beatles. Gladwell asks the question: What makes high-achievers different? The answers may surprise you.

CHAPTER 19: PROFESSIONAL HELP HELPS

Watch this: *https://www.youtube.com/watch?v=t2G8KVz-Twfw* The unforgettable story of Britain's 400m runner Derek Redmond, whose hamstring snapped during his event but was determined to finish the race at the Barcelona 1992 Olympic Games.

Read this: *Principles: Life & Work* by Ray Dalio. One of my favourites. Ray Dalio, one of the world's most successful investors and entrepreneurs, shares the unconventional principles that he's developed, refined, and used over the past forty years to create unique results in both life and business—and which any person or organization can adopt to help achieve their goals.

Read this: *Man's Search for Meaning* by Viktor Frankl. This seminal and bestselling book has been called "one of the great books of our time". In it, Frankl gives a riveting account of his time in the Nazi concentration camps and provides an insightful exploration of the human will to find meaning in spite of the worst adversity. This book will change you. It's a must read.

CHAPTER 21: TO DAUGHTERS

Read this: *https://www.betterhelp.com/advice/love/7-rea-sons-why-love-and-sex-go-together* Betterhelp.com is a really good online resource covering many topics. Check it out.

Read this: *The Five Love Languages* by Gary Chapman. Chapman identifies five basic "languages" of love and that all of us speak. He then helps couples learn to speak and understand their own, and their partners love language, and to effectively love and feel loved in return. It's a great book, and a real aha read for most men. It was for me!

Read this: *Wild at Heart Expanded Edition: Discovering the Secret of a Man's Soul* by John Eldredge. Somehow, some-where between childhood and the struggles of the daily grind, most men lose sight of their dreams. God made men to embrace a life of courage, adventure, and freedom, to take risks and find true purpose and belonging. This book invites men to recover their true heart.

CHAPTER 22: TO SONS

Read this: *Extreme Ownership. How US Navy Seals Lead and Win* by Jocko Willink and Leif Babin. This #1 bestseller describes many crucial leadership lessons distilled from the battlefield but equally applicable to many other facets of life and business.

CHAPTER 23: THERE'S SOMETHING BIGGER THAN YOU

Read this: *The Case for Christ: A Journalist's Personal Investigation of the Evidence for Jesus* by Lee Strobel. Is there credible evidence that Jesus really is the Son of God? Former atheist and investigative journalist Lee Strobel takes a look at the evidence from the fields of science, philosophy, and history.

Read this: *Evidence for the Historical Jesus: Is the Jesus of History the Christ of Faith?* by Gary R. Habermas. Habermas addresses the debate over the historical Jesus and shows a significant number of historical facts about Jesus in secular and non-New Testament sources that prove that the Jesus of history is the same Jesus of the Christian faith.